STAY ALIVE!

Survival Tactics for Hostages

To Patti,
May you never need this.
May you have it, if you do!

by

Robert K. Spear

Published by The Writers' Collective
Cranston, Rhode Island

To my wife, Barb, and to all our children. Thanks for your encouragement and support.

ISBN: 1-932133-21-6

Library of Congress Cataloging-in-Publication Data

Spear, Robert K.
Stay alive! : survival tactics for hostages / by Robert K. Spear.
p. cm.
Includes bibliographical references and index.
ISBN 1-932133-21-6 (alk. paper)
1. Hostages. 2. Hostages—Psychology. I. Title.
HV6571S66 2003
364.15'4—dc21

2003004391

Illustrations: Victor Brice

DISCLAIMER

Please note that the publisher and the authors of this instructional book are NOT RESPONSIBLE in any manner whatsoever for any injury or death which may occur after reading and following the instructions herein.

Published by
The Writers' Collective
Cranston, Rhode Island

Acknowledgements

Thanks to:

Birgit and Dean (models on the cover), Barb, Shanna, Desiree, and Candice (models for the Family photos). Thanks to Kurt Krueger for his fascinating true-life story. We really appreciate the critique, the support, and the new title from Lisa Grant of the Writers' Collective (www.writerscollective.org). We also appreciate the German translation and publishing of our first edition of *Surviving Hostage Situations* by Karl-Heintz Dissberger and his publishing company, Dissberger Verlag. Thanks to Joe and Ernest for their peer reviews.

About the Illustrator:

In 1988, US Army Specialist Victor Brice was the very talented part-time cartoonist who turned our action concepts into graphic representations.

ABOUT THE AUTHOR

Robert K. Spear

A seventh-degree back belt, Mr. Spear is know internationally as an American pioneer in the deadly Korean martial art of Hapkido. He was the first American to attain third-degree black belt and a letter of certification as an instructor from the Korea Hapkido Association in Seoul, Korea, in 1975. He is the past Chairman of the US Hapkido Federation's Board of Examiners. Mr. Spear has trained over 11,000 people in self-defense world-wide since 1974. He has written and produced numerous best-selling self-defense books and video training tapes.

A former US Army Intelligence Officer, Mr. Spear has presented papers at both the 1984 and 1988 Olympic Scientific Congress on martial art training experiments and physical conditioning experiments in both the US Army and his own Hapkido school. He has been published several times in a juried academic international physical education journal. He holds a BS in Orchestral Management (vocal concentration) from Indiana University and an MS in Business Administration from the University of Northern Colorado. He holds a State of Kansas Teacher's Certification in Choral, Band, and Orchestra.

In the 1990s, he was the deputy director of the Army's Deception Operations Office, US Army Combined Arms Center at Ft. Leavenworth, KS, and received the civil service equivalent to the Legion of Merit Medal for providing the concept paper upon which the strategy of the Gulf War was based. He has been a guest lecturer at both the Army and the Marine Command and General Staff Colleges, and the Army's prestigious post- CGSC School of Advanced Military Science. He and his wife, Barb, have owned The Book Barn in Leavenworth, Kansas since 1979 and Bob is currently the Publisher and Chief reviewer for Heartland Reviews (www.heartlandreviews.com).

In Memory of Col. D. Michael Moak (Deceased, 1998)

David Michael Moak, 47, an Army colonel and intelligence officer who was a specialist in counter-terrorism and the co-author with Mr. Spear of the book, *Surviving Hostage Situations*, died of a heart attack March 29, 1998 at the Walter Reed Army Medical Center. He lived in Centreville, Virginia.

Colonel Moak, a resident of the Washington area since 1994, was director of special activities in the office of the assistant secretary of defense for command, control, communications and intelligence. He had served in the Army since 1973, largely in infantry and intelligence posts.

He was a native of Baton Rouge, Louisiana, and a graduate of Southeastern Louisiana University. He received a master's degree in human resource management from Pepperdine University and a master's degree in national security strategy from the National Defense University. His overseas posts included Germany.

His honors included a Legion of Merit and Army Commendation Medal.
Survivors include his wife, Julia Moak, and two children, Aaron Moak and Shelane Moak, all of Centreville; his mother; and a brother.

TABLE OF CONTENTS

FOREWORD

Back in the summer of 1988 Major Mike Moak and I were relaxing at an organizational picnic in the American military housing area named Perlacher Forst in Munich, Germany. Mike had attended the Army's Command and General Staff College a couple of years before when I was working there as an Army civil servant at Fort Leavenworth, Kansas. We both came from military intelligence backgrounds, but Mike had recently transferred over to the new Special Operations branch of the Army. We began talking about hostage situations and the fact there was nothing available for potential victims to read. Until then all the books focused on the professional hostage negotiator.

Mike was the Assistant Brigade S-3, or plans and operations officer, and I was the Signals Intelligence and Electronic Warfare technical advisor to the 66th Military Intelligence Brigade. He had a strong background in counter-terrorism and I had a lot of experience with teaching self-defense and writing. We decided a book written to help potential victims was needed. After a careful review of the literature, we began to write. Mike wrote four of the chapters, which I rewrote to put into the same style as my seven chapters and the appendix. In the summer of 1989, I came home from Munich and picked up our first copies from the printer. This book, *Surviving Hostage Situations*, launched my new company, Universal Force Dynamics Publishing. Although a second edition came out in 1996, the only thing I changed was the price and some of the advertising material in the back of the book.

So much has happened since then — Desert Storm, the practice of carjacking, Waco, the Mura Federal Building bombing, Columbine and other school shootings, 9/11, the attack on Afghanistan, and the phrase, "going postal". As we sit poised to go to war with Iraq (I'm writing this the last week of January, 2003), many have become concerned about major terrorist retaliations from a wide variety of Middle Eastern countries and groups.

Unfortunately, Mike is no longer with us to provide any more input. Colonel D. Michael Moak collapsed on a treadmill in the Pentagon's athletic club with a massive heart attack in 1998. Machines prolonged his life for a week after that and then he migrated to a grave in the Arlington National Cemetery. It is so ironic that this All-American college quarterback, who kept himself totally fit throughout his career, passed on before my fat, crippled body decided to give up the ghost.

With the heightened awareness that hostage situations can happen anytime, anywhere and with the American public's concerns about a long, protracted conflict with fundamentalist Islamic forces, not to mention all the tragic hostage events which have made the news since the 1980s, I felt it was time to update *Surviving Hostage Situations*. Most of the old material has been included, but its relevancy to much which has taken place or may soon take place since the book's 1989 edition has been updated. On the advice of Lisa Grant of The Writers' Collective, I have also renamed the book, ***STAY ALIVE! Survival Tactics for Hostages***, as a more eye catching title.

I believe Mike's spirit sat on my shoulder during this process. He and I shared many of the same concerns and views for good people everywhere. It is with his spirit that I have taken on this revision in the hopes that it may save at least one or two more lives. God bless us all!

INTRODUCTION

Every week we hear news reports of someone being taken as a hostage. Sometimes terrorists are to blame, sometimes criminals or mentally disturbed people, and sometimes it's prison convicts. Whoever the captors are, it becomes readily apparent that the captives are people in the right place at the wrong time. It's one thing when people such as globetrotting executives, statesmen, intelligence operatives, journalists, and military personnel willingly accept a high probability of risk as a part of their job. They know the dangers, but by the very nature of their professions, feel as though the importance of their work justifies the risk of being captured. It's quite another thing to be a person on the street and to suddenly find yourself thrust into a hostage situation. Yet, that is happening more and more these days. People are being grabbed as hostages by escaping felons. They are being used as negotiating chips in prison riots. Others are being kidnapped for ransom or revenge and it doesn't always make sense as to who gets nabbed or why.

We can no longer afford to bury our heads in the sand about hostage taking. Not only has it become an everyday media phenomenon, hostage taking is pervasive among all stratas of society. No one is completely safe anymore!

The approach of this book is geared toward the average man and woman who might find themselves and their families in a hostage situation. It is a simple, specific guide as to who takes hostages and why, how to act if captured, and how to get away if an opportunity to do so arises. This book was written to provide you the tools necessary for you and your families to survive the dreadful experience of being taken hostage for whatever reason. As a bonus, you may find some of these tools useful for everyday living as well. Wherever possible, we have tried to use examples taken from actual hostage situations.

We are only sorry that others were unfortunate enough to have provided real life background material; therefore, we dedicate this book to those who have gone on before and to those who may need it in the future.

CHAPTER 1

THE HOSTAGE TAKERS

Who's at Risk?

Many of us don't like to think that bad things might happen to our families and ourselves. It's more comfortable to put such thoughts out of our minds. Most hope that if they don't think about it, it will never happen to them. This is a very common, normal attitude. It is because of this attitude; however, that the most common initial reaction to a hostage situation is total shock and disbelief. "This couldn't be happening to me!" the hostage thinks.

If we believe we'll never become a hostage, why read this book? The answer is because hostage-taking occurrences are steadily on the rise. What's more, we're finding out that everyone is more at risk than ever before. An unnamed government source tells usAl Queda training tapes instruct their terrorists to kill as many hostages as they can. Will you be one of the victims?

In 1981 a NATO Brigadier General, James Dozier, had been alerted by his Intelligence Staff that a terrorist kidnapping attempt on his person was imminent. Despite this forewarning, terrorists in the guise of Italian plumbers on an emergency call gained access to his quarters and spirited him away in a trunk.

The point is terrorists and criminals can take people hostage even if their victims are alert to the threat. This has been evident time after time in Lebanon where hostages were taken despite the use of all the standard preventative measures.

These examples are highly dramatic because of the intense media coverage that is usually given to terrorist situations. The taking of hostages, however, is actually commonplace. There are stories almost daily about criminals taking a hostage to provide them protection as a body shield, or an estranged parent taking hostages of the rest of the family to gain attention or revenge, or rioting convicts taking hostages for many of the same reasons that terrorists take hostages.

The public is bombarded with news stories about all kinds of hostage situations.

In fact the media seems to take almost ghoulish delight in presenting these stories with the air of soap operas. There is a significant morbid interest factor that captures the man-on-the-street's imagination. Many people inevitably identify with the hostages and wonder what they would do if they ever found themselves in the same type of situation. Surviving Hostage Situations will provide you with detailed answers to these questions.

This book gives specific guidance and examples of what to expect and what to do in any kind of hostage situation in order to survive in the best manner possible. It is written for those in traditionally high-risk occupations (journalists, businessmen, diplomats, soldiers, police officers, prison administrators, etc.) and for the general public, which is now considered to be at almost as great a risk as the above professions.

Since anyone could end up becoming a hostage, it might be wise to know something about those people who do the hostage taking. We will examine:

- Terrorists
- Assorted Criminals
- And a special class of criminal hostage taker — the Prison Convict

Terrorists

It's been said that terrorism is the poor man's war. If you

don't have the money to field an Army in support of your cause, use economical terrorist tactics. Instead of trying to take over a government directly, the terrorist tries to demonstrate that the government is powerless, unable to protect its citizens. If this can be accomplished, the result is a loss of confidence by the average citizen in the government's competence and resolve.

Constant terrorist attacks produce shock at first, which soon transcends into anger and criticism at the government for not stopping or preventing the terrorist attacks. Once the terrorists can achieve this state of mind in the populace, they go after what they actually want — the consideration of their demands, especially their political ones. The media will usually press for the government to consider the terrorists' claims.

[1] "This is a no-lose proposition for the terrorists. If the government does not give in, the terrorist promises (and often delivers) further terrorism. This induces further criticism of the government and more, increasingly desperate calls to heed the terrorist demands. If the government succumbs, the terrorist scores an obvious victory; even if the terrorist agrees to a temporary hiatus (which he seldom does), the citizen knows that his government has caved in and betrayed his trust yet again.... Once the line of concession is crossed, more atrocities and more demands are sure to follow."

[2] Terrorist strategy is based upon the capacity to strike future blows, no matter what. The terrorist goal is not negotiation but capitulation by the government. One often-used tactic to obtain this goal is the taking of hostages. In counter terrorism parlance, the government or authority structure is the primary victim. The secondary victim is the hostage. (Try telling that to the hostage). Terrorists take hostages to draw attention to their cause and to confound the authorities.

So, who are these people who fight governments and rob innocent citizens of their freedom and safety? Lets examine the following aspects of their profile:

- Age
- Religion
- Politics/Ideology
- Sex
- Sanity
- Thrill Seeking
- Background

- Will-To-Kill
- Revenge
- Self-Destruction (Death-Wish)
- Networking
- An Unusual Support Base

Age

Terrorist training can start at a young age. Bob Spear knows an Iranian family who escaped from the Khomeini regime. Their youngest son told of receiving street fighting, marksmanship, and bomb making instructions in Middle School (Junior High School) classes in Tehran. Terrorist groups often like to get 15-20 year old youths into their training programs because that is the most idealistic/romantic age group. Teenagers are much easier to mold and much more adventurous than people 10 to 20 years their senior. This age group can be convinced it's glorious to die for their cause. One of the reasons the Iranian family escaped when they did was because the Mullahs had commenced drafting Middle School students into the Iranian Revolutionary Army. These students went straight to the front lines with little or no training to clear paths through Iraqi minefields with their bodies. This enabled the older foot soldiers to commit their attack—unbloodied and fresh — while the younger boys lay dead and wounded, a sacrifice to the Shi'ite cause. Iran lost the better part of a male generation in this manner.

Iranians aren't the only ones to callously use their youth. The Viet Cong would use young teenagers as their rank and file and even children for special missions. Many an American veteran still has nightmares about killing a child wearing a satchel charge and running toward him.

The Irish Republican Army has used children in the role of spotters, spies, and couriers. The PLO uses youths to hurl rocks at Israeli soldiers to draw their rifle fire in retaliation. The PLO actually wants casualties amongst their youth to draw attention and sympathy from a worldwide audience.

So, many terrorists start their training and mind-conditioning at an early age. What does this mean to you, the potential hostage? Simply put, the terrorists are true believers in their causes. They may not want to die but are willing to do so if that is what is required. Hostage taking missions are generally not spur-of-the moment occurrences, but are highly structured, well planned operations. The personnel involved are selected for both their skills and especially for their commitment. Although your abductors may be in their early to mid-twenties, they have a century of training and experience behind them.

Religion

Religious training and commitment are the norm for many terrorists since many have causes based upon religious grounds. Whether it be Irish Catholics seeking separation from Protestant rule or Shi'ite Moslems fighting for a Palestinian State and against Sunni Moslem domination, many have strong convictions. In each case, their end justifies the means; the cause justifies the ethic. After all, some of the bloodiest wars in history have been fought over religious differences. Why should a war of terrorism be any different?

Politics/Ideology

Although many terrorist movements are based upon religion, many are also based upon political or ideological platforms. Communism is the most commonly heard language among these groups; however, this is due more to the training and support given by Communistic regimes than it is out of Marxist commitment. Far more powerful and common forces are the ideologies of nationalism and tribalism. These are the driving forces behind African terrorist movements as well as the Basque, Croatian, and Armenian causes. Xenophobia (the fear of outsiders and those not like ourselves) is a strong motivating force. If you are not a member of your captors' group or nationality, don't expect their sympathy at first. You are going to have to remind them of attributes you have in common with them later on, so they will begin to see you as a fellow human and not as a faceless nonentity.

Sex

Ah, the ultimate attention-getting word. In this case, we wish to discuss two aspects of terrorism's sexual involvement:

- Female Captors
- Sexual Practices

Female Captors

It is increasingly common to find women throughout the rank and file and the mid-level management levels of terrorist organizations. Numerous skyjacking incidents have included women hostage takers. They have been used to carry weapons through airports' security or to distract security guards. Some have been leaders or co-leaders of hostage-taking missions. A Palestinian woman, Dalal Mughrabi, led the 1978 PLO raid on Israel. The Lod airport massacre was led by a Japanese Red Army female named Fusako Shigenobu who was a major terrorist trainer and manager within the PLO. A German woman was a co-leader of the Entebbe skyjacking incident. Ulrike Meinhof was a co-founder and the real power behind the infamous German Baeder-Meinhof gang. The American Weather Underground organization was led by Bernardine Dohn, and the Symbionese Liberation Army had a majority of women members. Even Al Queda has started to recruit woman.

Why all the female involvement? For one thing, as mentioned above, women have unique utility as distracters and couriers. For another, many of these women have something to prove. Most are ardent feminists. In fact, the most dangerous, most macho-acting hostage takers tend to be women. They intimidate male negotiators in hostage situations. They are far more likely to use harsh violence than their male counterparts because they feel that they have to prove their commitment and capabilities are above reproach. If you find yourself in a hostage situation with female involvement, be extremely careful not to antagonize them; it could be fatal.

Sexual Practices

Terrorist acts such as hostage taking involve great power trips. Violence and anti-establishment acts are aphrodisiacal to some people. Many who knew Andreas Baeder and Ulrike Meinhof say that Baeder's primary interest in the movement was based more on available free sex than it was on ideological commitment. There is also a strong connection between the act of killing and sexual excitement. Some people get "turned on" by torturing and killing other humans. One of the most heinous pornographic film categories is the "Snuff" movie where a film was made of an actual rape ending with the victim's real death. As society becomes more decadent, such deplorable acts become more commonplace. In a related aspect, some terrorists evolve from committed ideologues to depraved violent sex seekers. Again, watch out for this personality amongst your captors. They love to hear their victims plead and beg (an act which heightens their turn-on). Try to remain non-emotional and low-key around them. Don't be obviously brave, but don't be overtly afraid either. Detachment is probably the safest reaction.

The Iraqi Army is said to have Rape Units, which have been used to systematically rape Khurdish women to obtain information and confessions from their men. This is of concern if any of our female soldiers become POWs in any conflict with Iraq.

Sanity

One might think that a terrorist who commits violent, despicable acts could not be completely sane; however, if we consider that most nations require soldiers to commit similar acts for the common-good of their citizens, that view doesn't track. You don't have to be insane to commit acts of force and violence; you just have to have a strong enough cause driving your actions.

In fact, most terrorist organizations want troops who are in control of their emotions and actions. The previously mentioned sexual-violence pathology could be a distracter or disrupter of a well-planned hostage situation.

One pathology that may be common in experienced terrorists is that of paranoia. Months or years of living in a shadow world, worrying about capture and death may cause them to balance fear with a driving sense of mission.

Another observed personality quirk is that of a split personality (schizophrenia) which may be gentle and caring one minute and a stone-killer the next. Again, this may be a coping mechanism that overbalances the requirement to be brutal and cruel with an overly developed sense of sympathy. The appearance of hail-fellow-well-met normalcy is absolutely essential so that terrorists will safely intermingle with everyday society. This is one way in which they can live their front while compartmentalizing their "dark-side" until it's needed.

Thrill Seeking

One might think that the typical terrorist would be an excitement freak; however, this is not usually the case for those who would be professionals.

[3] "While some US and Western European students-cum-terrorists may act out secret fantasies of strength, domination, and danger through acts of terrorism, the great majority of recruits inducted into the ranks of terrorist organizations in Algeria, Kenya, Malaysia, the Philippines, Cyprus, Ireland, and the Middle East (both Zionist and Palestinian organizations) became terrorists as a matter of circumstance, not because of some defective dimension of their personality or to satisfy cravings for thrill or danger."

In fact, there is very little excitement in a terrorist's life. Except for the hard training (which wears old rather quickly), the only real excitement is the latter planning stages and the actual mission. The rest of the time is spent trying to blend into the flow of community life around them.

Many terrorists, especially Western European ones, take jobs, live in clean, quiet neighborhoods, drive inconspicuous cars, and are excellent neighbors. They do this to insure their personal survival. The Al Queda terrorists pretended to be lapsed Islamics — womanizing and bar drinking to blend in with the American culture. They justified their "sinning" by believing Allah would forgive all because they were sinning to further his cause.

In America we often take our freedoms for granted; however, in most of Europe, everyone carries an ID card and reports to the nearest police station as soon as they move into a neighborhood. If they don't, the police will be around to see them shortly after they move in with very little in the way of a sense of humor. Also, many retired pensioners, with little else but time on their hands, like to keep a watch on everything that goes on in the neighborhood — a crime watch by a bunch of little old ladies in tennis shoes.

Given this type of a controlled environment, a terrorist is wise to appear outwardly as a model citizen until it's time to move on. This does not make for a very exciting life; however, the terrorist act is so excitement-filled that it can make up for an awful lot of ennui.

Gayle Rivers, the pseudonym for the counter-terrorist author of "The War Against Terrorists: How To Win It", says, [4] "In my experience, terrorism is addictive. Terrorists get to like their work more and more. They get a high from making plans for an outrage, they get a high from the actual commission of an act that immediately grabs the world's attention, and they get a high when important governments literally let them get away with murder and help their leaders escape the law."

Background

Terrorists come from all walks of life. Some of the worst have come from very affluent backgrounds. Social class does not seem to have nearly as much effect as does past negative experiences or training during their impressionable years. Many have had an unhappy childhood with feelings of inadequacy, helplessness, or impersonality. Consider the ultimate terrorist, Adolf Hitler, who parlayed an unhappy childhood and the rejection as an artist by Jewish professors into a series of terrorist attacks which came close to conquering all of Europe.

5 "According to some psychiatrists, the individual who is completely unaccepted and unloved has the choice of either rejecting himself or rejecting the group or society that he believes has judged him wrong. Western terrorist movements, moreover, are full of male and female achievers who fall short of their personal goals and expectations and blame society for their shortcomings."

There is an aspect of class in terrorist organizations in that the rank and file membership tends to be drawn from the population from whence it came. For example, the IRA tends to come from the working class. The German, Italian, Japanese, and Palestinian terrorists come from middle class backgrounds. The American Weathermen came from white middle or upper class environments.

6 "Phillip A. Karber has often observed that historically the most dangerous and successful urban terrorism movements have been waged not by a band of desperate intellectuals, but by a highly organized movement incorporating the technical skills and dogged determination found among the blue collar workers and lower echelon middle class."

Will To Kill

What are your chances of getting killed as a terrorist's hostage? All we can say is, "It depends!" If you stay quiet, maintaining a low profile during the beginning of the incident, you may have a pretty good chance of coming through it alive and well. You should be aware, however, that terrorists often will commit a token murder or two. Gayle Rivers talks about how terrorist skyjackers take control of their airline passengers as quickly and completely as possible.

7 "... it is important to remember that the terrorists' adrenaline high incorporates their fear, and that is what leads to the sacrificial first killing of a passenger. They have been instructed to avoid overkill. But they are encouraged by their mentors to make the sacrificial killing brutal in order to derive maximum benefit from the act. Nobody wants to be killed. Nobody wants to be killed like that. A planeload of normal human beings, frightened as never before in their lives, is transformed into a fuselage full of sheep

ready to do the terrorists' bidding."

On the other hand, if you are argumentative or if you try to fight, you may be signing your own death warrant. It's a lot easier to brutally murder someone if that person has just angered or frightened you. Remember, the terrorists are seeking a sacrificial lamb which is a doctrinally standard act for them to commit in order to gain immediate control. Don't encourage them to single you out. Not all terrorists are natural killers. Most people can kill if their lives or their friends' lives depend on it; however, to kill a defenseless hostage in cold blood is much harder to do. The nearer the physical distance between the killer and the victim, the harder it is, psychologically, to kill him. It's easier to plant a bomb and leave it without personally viewing the havoc caused than it is to put a gun to someone's head and pull the trigger. Understanding this, there are a number of extremist terrorist groups in the past that required a recruit to personally murder a member of their opposition before they were allowed full membership rights in the movement. The Mau Maus went beyond even this by requiring cannibal acts of their prospective members.

Once the personal killing line is crossed; however, it often becomes easier to commit further murders. As Rivers said, terrorism is addictive. Fortunately, not many are able to do this.

Revenge

This may become the most common drive behind future terrorist hostage situations involving Americans. If we go to war with Iraq and it stretches out over time, look to see all kinds of revenge motivated attacks on our homeland.

Self Destruction

A committed terrorist, a true believer, is willing to die for his or her cause. Therefore, terrorists often succeed with their mission when other, less ardent fighters would have fallen back. This attitude, the essence of terrorism, makes it so effective. They say they are willing to die so that the people they are fighting for may be better off. Psychiatrists, however, say there is a darker reason for this fatalistic fanaticism, namely unquenchable thirst for recognition through martyrdom. Many, in fact, are self-destructive. Look at the 9/11 terrorists who sacrificed their lives to bring down the World Trade Center and the Pentagon. Not only were the hostages on board the planes at risk from the terrorists, but in the future, they will be at risk from governmental air forces who will shoot down a passenger plane before it can be used as a weapon against important targets.

Networking

There are many types of terrorist organizations — some are religion based, some right wing, some left wing, some communist based, and some are nationalistic. Yet, regardless of their driving causes, many are assisting one another. Japanese are attacking Israeli targets in support of the PLO. Germans are providing explosives and Italians are providing Mafia-produced triggering devices for the IRA to use against the British. The North Koreans are providing trainers and operatives to the highest bidder. Money for various operations is provided by various so-called humanitarian organizations such as the American-Irish NORAID funds.

8 "What links the individuals in all the terrorist groups around the world is their distaste for the democratic process, their intense hatred of their perceived enemies. Their common desire is to disestablish the Western democracies, especially America because of its leadership role. And finally, what links them together is their obsession with violence against human beings, shootings, maiming, blowing up. The terrorist act becomes their religion. They can, therefore, link hands and arms and funds with the like-minded."

Warning: An Unusual Support Base

In addition to the interconnected support agreements amongst the various terrorist organizations and terrorist-supporting countries, there is a little-known practice that is causing concern in several Western Intelligence circles. Third World terrorists and criminals are beginning to take advantage of Western society's more traditional support systems. Bob, a member of the Church of Jesus Christ of Latter Day Saints (the Mormons), has personally experienced this practice on two different occasions — once in the US and once in Germany. Christian religious organizations who are known to be unquestioningly supportive of members and even nonmembers in need are being used as free, safe refuges for terrorists and criminals in transit and by Third World operatives to infiltrate American communities.

Professing Christians like to help those in distress, especially if they espouse the same beliefs that we support. Knowing this, these unscrupulous individuals are approaching local wards and congregations with plausible stories of hard luck and are bartering their need and supposed membership for free room and board for a few nights with member-families. They sometimes seek good jobs and social acceptance so they will blend in with the community. There is even a concern that certain international organizations such as the Boy Scouts, the Girl Scouts, and the Red Cross are being used as well.

Some of these people have been found with blank organizational forms which they fill out to support whatever cover story they are using as required. BE CAREFUL! The guy you give shelter to today may be taking someone hostage tomorrow. Do not blindly accept a form or a membership card. Ask questions that only a member in good standing would know the answers to and listen carefully for inconsistencies. If there is any doubt in your mind, politely refer them to the governmental welfare agencies in the area and stay out of any further entanglements.

Conclusions

In general, don't take chances with terrorists. They're highly motivated professionals and will kill in self-defense or to make a point. Try to stay calm and quiet, follow instructions, and try not to draw attention to yourself. Wait to see what happens!

Criminals

This next section deals with three types of criminal hostage takers:

- Escaping Felons
- The Emotionally / Mentally Disturbed
- Kidnappers
- Carjackers
- School Students and Fellow Employees

Escaping Felons

Probably the most common occurrence of criminal hostage taking and the one most likely to happen to the person-on-the-street involves escaping felons. The three most common places people are grabbed as hostages are banks, liquor stores, and convenience stores. In almost all cases, a robber either panics or is interrupted in the act of his crime by an alarm or by the police. The thief reacts with fear of injury and loss of freedom. To increase his safety, security, and his possibilities for escape, he grabs someone standing nearby, threatens him or her with a weapon, and drags the hostage along as a body shield. Another common scenario is for a robber without a getaway car to halt traffic and climb into a vehicle taking the driver and/or passengers hostage.

Of the two situations, the second is potentially more dangerous because of the likelihood of high-speed chases and the opportunity to get away from the authorities. This may put the hostage in grave danger later on when the felon feels safe and has more time to think and act. If a male robber abducts a female, often times he will rape and sometimes kill her. I will cover this later under the carjacking paragraph.

In the first case, inside a building or on the way out, the police have a better chance to contain the situation and can immediately begin to negotiate.

The key to your safety as a hostage is based upon the kind of criminal involved, his experience level, and whether mood altering substances are present. If the felon is relatively inexperienced, he is more likely to panic and do something dangerous or stupid. Most experienced thieves will be more likely to release hostages and surrender once the situation has stabilized to the point they are no longer afraid of being shot out-of-hand by an overzealous policeman or proprietor.

Drug addicts in need of a fix are very dangerous because they are physically shaky, nervous wrecks, and extremely impatient. If they have taken Speed (amphetamines) or Angel Dust (PCP) to enhance their confidence, anything could happen. Angel Dust is especially bad because people under its influence become super strong, super fast, and super violent. Bob saw one incident which required eight big Military Policemen to subdue one medium-sized soldier who was high on Angel Dust and began freaking out. Since the PCP high cancels all pain signals and natural subconscious force-governors, the user is very difficult to control. Bob advises his security guard students that the best way to deal with one of these "berserkers" when there is not enough manpower present is to forget attacking painful nerve centers and try to take away his mechanical supports by breaking his collar bones and knees so he can't use his limbs. He won't feel the pain, but his limbs will not be able to perform their normal functions of grabbing, striking, or kicking.

Emotionally/Mentally Disturbed

So many crimes of violence are crimes of passion. The one call that the police hate most to answer is the domestic squabble. Anything is liable to happen when a distraught husband, wife, or spouse equivalent has a falling out with the partner and takes the partner and/or the children hostage. There is a lot of anger and pent-up frustration present in these situations. Often revenge is a motive for taking former loved ones hostage. If you are a spouse being held hostage, you would be much better off to allow an outside, uninvolved police negotiator to plead your case. Any talking on your part with the hostage taker will only serve to antagonize him. Answer his questions unemotionally, being careful not to argue, and keep quiet the rest of the time.

The same advice also holds true for non-domestic hostage situations involving mentally disturbed hostage takers. Again, these incidents are especially dangerous. Disturbed individuals are not rational or predictable. Some may be listening to and obeying voices that no one else can hear. Others may be suicidal and wouldn't mind taking a few people along for company in death. Let the outside experts try to handle the negotiations and stay out of the way if you can. We'll address more on this in Chapter Three.

Kidnappers

These are the most dangerous of all the criminals in that they have everything to gain and very little to lose by killing you. Kidnappers are not like terrorists who take hostages to draw attention to themselves and their cause, thereby bringing embarrassment to the ruling government. Kidnappers want everything kept quiet. They desire no confrontation with the authorities. They especially want anonymity so they can enjoy their anticipated ransom profits in peace. If the victim is the only one who can identify them, they're likely to kill him. Again, this is different than terrorist kidnappers who take hostages repeatedly. In those cases, they will almost always release their victims for ransom so they will be assured of getting ransom payments for later victims. The criminal, however, doesn't have these organizational political support systems to insure his continued security and safety.

If you are a criminal's kidnap victim, emphasize that you don't want to know who he is or what he looks like. If you can't identify him later on, you'll have a better chance of being spared.

Carjackers

In addition to criminals using a hostage and her car as a means of escaping a crime scene, is the far to common carjacking criminal. Why? Because the car companies and devices like **The Club™** have made car stealing almost impossible. New steering wheel locking systems, new car alarms, engine cutoff devices and digital keying systems have made it very hard to steal cars. The hotwire days are over. The car theft guys have been forced to go after a softer target — YOU! Rather than boosting your wheels while the car is unattended, they prefer grabbing you along with the car for fun and recreational purposes. The carjackers say, "Hey, I can steal any type of car I want without damaging it. I can get the car keys which probably have the house keys on the ring too. I can rob the driver, and I can do anything with her or him I want — maybe even rip off their house or apartment in the process. What a deal!"

We will address more on this in later chapters. Suffice it to say you'll be dealing with some very desperate characters.

School Students / Fellow Employees

These hostage takers are certainly disturbed, but they're not necessarily crazy. One thing about Columbine that surprised me was that we hadn't seen it happening before. Kids can be incredibly cruel to one another. If you've never been on the receiving end of the majority of a schools student body's contempt, you don't know how pervasive of a downer that can be. It's one thing to take on a bully or two; it's quite another to receive slings and barbs from almost everyone you know. You just can't fight and win. You're damned if you do and damned if you don't. The same sort of situation can happen on the job. A person locked into a never-ending round of poor treatment day after day by his peers and superiors must either try to escape it, or they may go "Postal" — flipping out violently over even the smallest of slights, which just happened to push the person over the edge.

When that time comes, anything can happen. The jilted boy wants to prove to the girl what a bad decision she made. The passed-over employee wants justice. All the Jocks must die. The reasons are almost endless. These hostage takers are some of the most dangerous because of their highly charged emotions.

Convicts and Prisoners

There are two types of situations in which convicts might take one hostage:

- Prison Riots
- Prisoner Escapes

Prison Riots

Convicts normally riot for better treatment, better conditions, for revenge, and out of fear. The first three are self-explanatory. The fourth, fear, was really brought home during the Atlanta prison riots, which were sparked by Cuban Boat People criminals who were afraid they would be sent back to Cuba. The Cubans panicked and were finally calmed by assurances they would not be shipped home.

People at risk during prison riots are the prison administration, guards, visitors, and other prisoners. Riots are generally very violent — a lot of grudges get settled quickly. After all, where there are proven killers with nothing to lose, death stalks the confinement area. Imagine how a guard felt in a New Mexico State prison, when a homicidal maniac came to tell him that later on he would kill the guard. To prove his intent was serious, he came back a couple of hours later carrying the head of another prisoner who had also on his grievance list. Hostage situations can't get more mentally traumatic than that. Fortunately counter-riot forces rescued the guard before the prisoner could make good on his promise.

Convicts can be animals — capable of the most heinous acts. The last thing you'll ever want to be is a hostage inside prison walls, because hostages do get killed and rescuers must storm a fortress to get in. Keeping a low profile and hiding are the keys to survival. Also, gaining the protection of a less violent prisoner faction can be helpful.

Prison Escapes

Both Mike Moak and Bob Spear have lived in Prison City U.S.A. — Leavenworth, Kansas. This is a lovely, sophisticated, intellectual Midwest town of 50,000+ inhabitants. Its primary industries are two large Hallmark Card factories, the US. Army's Combined Arms Center with the Army's Command and General Staff College, and seven prisons — the Fort Leavenworth Military Disciplinary Barracks, the Leavenworth Federal Penitentiary (including the "Big House" and a minimum security prison camp), a Kansas State Penitentiary for men, a contractor-run Federal Marshals' holding facility, and the Leavenworth County Jail with a small juvenile detention facility next door.

Prison escapes don't happen often, but they do happen. It is a constant factor to be considered because I live here. Now, the first thing you should understand is that there is little cause for worry, because escaping prisoners usually try to put as much distance between them and the town as quickly as possible. The people who usually have more to fear are in the towns ten or twenty miles away, because that is where escapees usually stop for provisions, vehicles, and sometimes hostages.

In this case, the risk to the man-on-the-street is much greater than in a prison riot. If escapees invade your home or vehicle, don't try to fight them (they're desperate at this stage). Give them what they want and send them on their way. If they want to take you along as a hostage, claim to have a medical condition which might slow them down. Hopefully they will be too interested in traveling quickly to bother with you. If they do take you, constantly think of escape and make your break at the first chance because you are in grave danger. Try to communicate by tapping out SOS (3 shorts, 3 longs, and 3 shorts) on the brake peddle. If you stop for gas, try to leave a note in the bathroom or on the gas cap. Try to speed or disobey other traffic laws when near police cars — anything to draw attention from the authorities. If the situation deteriorates while you're driving, try to crash and run away.

Summary

There are a significant number of hostages taken every year, and there are many types of hostage takers. Understand who they are (terrorists, criminals, or convicts) and use the knowledge within the rest of this book to help you survive if you're ever taken hostage.

[1] Benjamin Netanyahu, *Terrorism: How the West Can Win the Global Battle*, The Jonathan Institute, 1986, P. 201.

[2] Neal C. Livingston, *The War Against Terrorism*, D. C. Heath and Co., 1982, P. 31-55.

[3] Ibid. P. 33.

[4] Gayle Rivers, *The War Against Terrorists: How To Win It*, Stein and Doubleday Publishers, 1986, P. 11.

[5] Livingston, P.37.

[6] Livingston, P- 39-40

[7] Rivers, P. 60-61.

[8] Ibid., P. 98.

CHAPTER 2

HOSTAGE SITUATIONS

History

It is interesting to note that the dictionary defines hostage as, [1] "a person given or held as security for the performance of certain actions, promises, etc., by another." In medieval times the exchange of hostages was a common practice. Peace treaties and oaths of loyalty were bound by the giving of hostages. The usual custom was for the Lord making the promise to hand over a member(s) of his immediate family to the other ruler. If he went back on his word, the hostages' lives were forfeit.

Actually, the life of a hostage in those days wasn't too bad. Having no real day-to-day responsibilities, they usually had the run of the castle and its surrounding countryside. Their only serious concern was that someone back home might fail to honor their side of the agreement. Often a young son or daughter would be sent as a hostage. They would grow up alongside the children of the hostage-keeping ruler — studying from the same teachers, playing games together, hunting, and other normal activities practiced by their class. Later on, after they were returned to their home court, they would bring a unique insight into future relations with their former keepers.

Now, of course, the word hostage has much more negative connotations. It is used to describe someone taken against his will, placed in danger, and used as a helpless pawn in political and criminal power plays. Let us examine modern hostage taking from the aspects of how these incidents develop and their components. We will address:

- Kidnapping defined
- Hostage taking preparations
- The four phases of a hostage incident
- Typical hostage-taking locations

Kidnapping Defined

Kidnapping is a tactic used primarily by terrorists and criminals as a means of obtaining money through ransom. Kidnappings have other benefits too, such as:

- providing publicity,
- obtaining the release of jailed comrades,
- forcing large foreign corporations which have been frequently hit by kidnappings to leave the country, and
- forcing a government into granting concessions.

The major difference between a kidnapping and any other kind of hostage taking situation is that the kidnapper hides his victim while the other hostage takers confront the authorities with their victims.

Kidnapping requires extensive planning and precise execution in both the seizure and holding phases, which we will discuss in more detail later. The two primary methods that kidnappers use to accomplish a kidnapping are to take the victim from a static location, such as the victim's office or residence, or to kidnap the victim enroute, either when he's on foot or in a vehicle.

Static Location

In order to take the victim from a static location, the kidnapper must know: the location; what security measures are employed; what time the victim is at the location; how aware the victim and his family, friends, and associates are; and the number, times, and routines of police and/or guard patrols in the area.

To gain this information, the kidnappers will survey the location and area and make dry runs to find the best way to penetrate the location. The kidnappers will use ploys and ruses to penetrate the location. Ploys and ruses used in the past have included:

- repairman,
- salesman,
- survey-taker,
- policeman,

- mailman,
- deliveryman,
- business appointments cleared for access,
- requests to use the phone,
- requests for information,
- and surreptitious entry.

Brigadier General Dozier's home was reconnoitered by a single individual posing as a metermaid. If Mrs. Dozier had only been aware of the utility company's policy of sending meter readers out in pairs, she may have become suspicious.

The actions for a kidnapping from a static location include:

- penetrate the location,
- gain control of the victim,
- remove the victim from the location,
- and escape without being detected.

Brigadier General Dozier's kidnapping was a classic static site operation. Terrorists entered his quarters posing as plumbers. The story they used to gain entry was they were checking a leak in the apartment below his and wanted to see if the leak was originating from his apartment. General Dozier believed their story and let them in. The terrorists gained control of General Dozier by force and by threats against his wife. He was drugged, placed in a large box, and carried out of his quarters. The terrorists escaped with General Dozier in a van, leaving Mrs. Dozier bound and gagged, locked in the laundry room to ensure they would escape undetected.

Enroute

In order to kidnap a victim enroute, the kidnappers must know the victim's routine. Once a routine has been established, the kidnappers can plan an attack to include a time and an attack site. The steps in kidnapping a victim enroute are:

- select and identify the victim,
- gather intelligence concerning the victim's vehicle and/or travel routines (to include times and routes),
- select an attack site along the route,
- and select a time of attack based upon the victim's routines and the patterns of the police's security patrols.

It's fairly simple to take a victim on foot enroute once his routines are determined so that a day, time, and place can be selected. The kidnappers will then gain control of the victim, throw him into a vehicle, and drive away to the holding area.

The scenario for taking a victim from a vehicle is:

- isolate the attack site and stop the vehicle,
- gain control over the victim,
- and escape.

Every kidnapping incident in which the victim is taken from a vehicle follows this scenario. Any difference will come in the ploy or ruse followed by the kidnappers to isolate the attack site and to stop the vehicle. Ploys and ruses used previously to stop vehicles include:

- roadblocks,
- accidents,
- hitchhikers,
- ramming,
- police disguises,
- and by pushing bicycles or baby carriages in front of the vehicle.

To isolate or secure the attack site, kidnappers have called security forces prior to the attack to tie up the phone lines, used fake police roadblocks and accidents as diversion tactics. A classic example of a kidnapping while enroute in a vehicle was the case of German industrialist, Hans Martin Schleyer. In kidnapping Herr Schleyer, the Red Army Faction used roadblocks and telephone calls to isolate and secure the area. A stationary vehicle was used

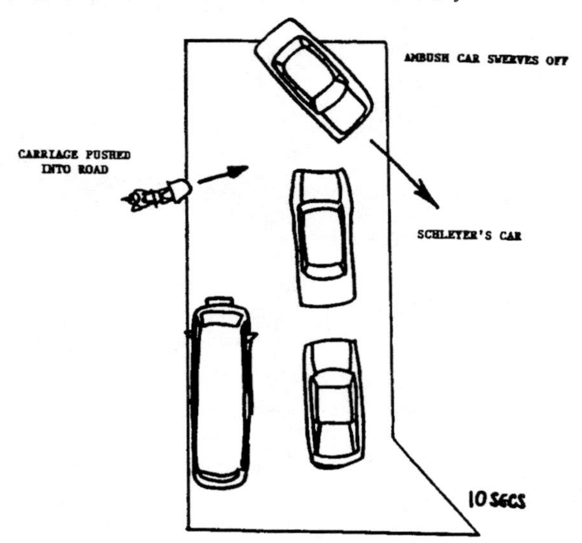

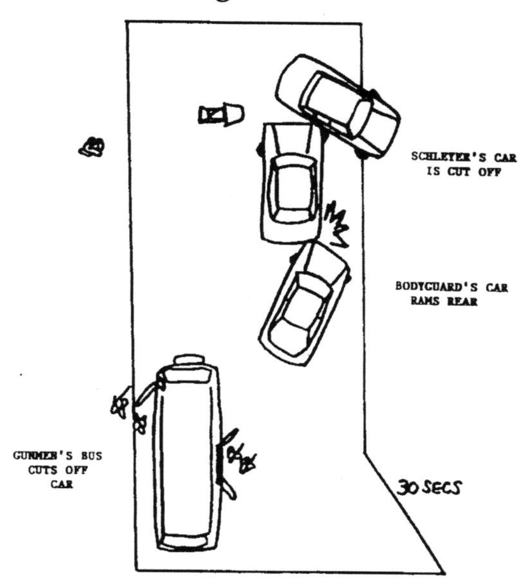

to channel Schleyer's vehicle and the security chase car. A woman rolling a baby carriage and a moving taxicab were used to cause Schleyer's chase vehicle to pin his car in. The following illustrations show how incredibly fast this incident was and how each aspect of it proceeded.

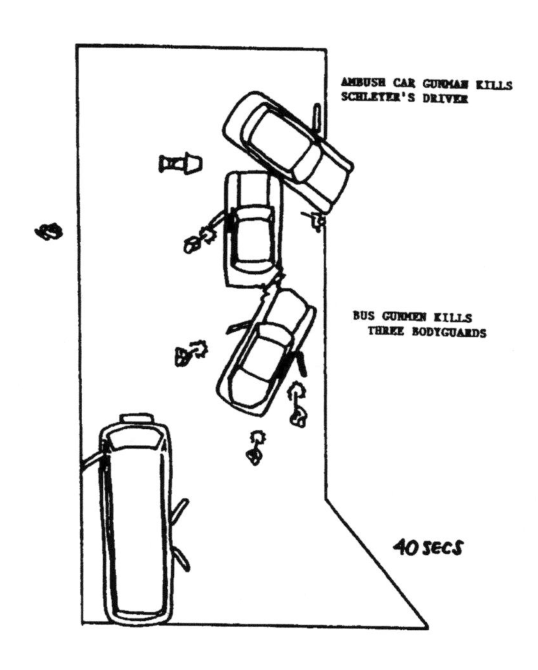

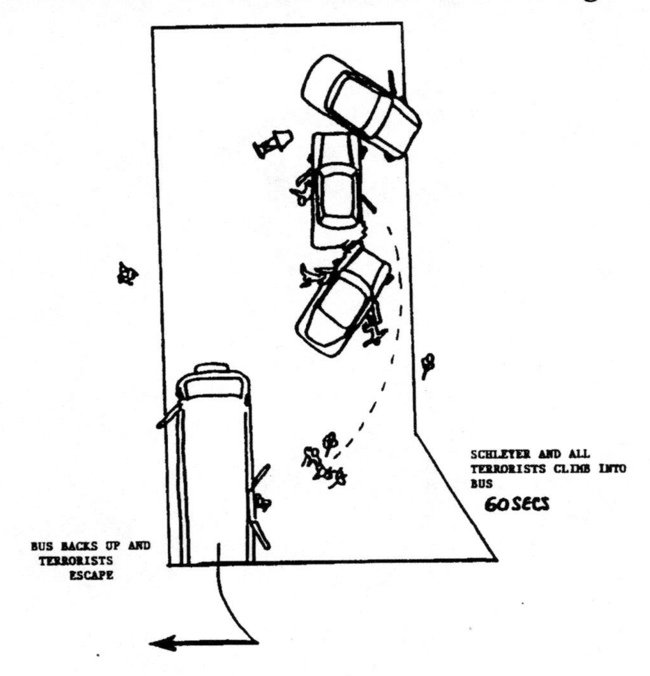

Pre-Incident Preparations

The criminal hostage taker (excepting the convict and the kidnapper) generally does not have enough time to prepare prior to the hostage incident. Most of these scenarios evolve as happenstance situations with little or no previous planning. Terrorists and kidnappers; however, usually go through elaborate preparation rituals prior to their taking of hostages.

In this pre-incident phase, the would-be abductors determine what they hope to gain from a hostage situation- ransom, political concessions, media attention, or whatever. Terrorist groups are especially professional in their approach to incident preparation. Preoperational activities are meticulously planned. Reconnaissance missions are conducted against the intended target (the potential hostage) and/or the areas of future operations by small, special intelligence teams. The leaders of the terrorist group then conceive and prepare the detailed plans for the upcoming operation based upon the information gathered by these special teams.

For security reasons, often planners, reconnaissance teams, and the actual abduction team will never meet. Information and orders are passed along through intermediaries, liaison sections, or by message drops. Training and rehearsals sometimes take place in countries outside the target area. Perpetrators, even the leaders, often have no knowledge of which specific target will be taken until it is time to conduct the operation. If a primary target is unavailable, or the risk is perceived as too great, an alternative target is selected. Most terrorist contingency plans include alternate targets. The plan may also include alternative negotiation demands and departure or escape routes.

Although most criminal kidnappers do not have this much organizational support, the real pros will go through a similar process within the scope of their particular capabilities. The kidnapper, however, will not generally have alternative victims.

Phases of Hostage Situations

There are four phases of hostage incidents acknowledged by most subject area experts:

- the capture
- transport/consolidation
- holding
- termination

Capture Phase

In terrorist situations, the strike team is brought together

The Capture

and briefed on the specific primary and alternate targets. They conduct final rehearsals to fine-tune the operation, move to the attack site, and then carry out the plan. Once commenced, the action is at the point of no return and will continue on through to its natural consequence. Kidnappings by criminals start similarly but with less emphasis on security and support.

Ordinary criminals and emotionally disturbed hostage takers generally spend little or no time on preparation but find themselves taking hostages as a matter of necessity or inspiration rather than as the natural outcome of some elaborate plan.

Convicts, on the other hand, may fit into either scenario depending on the spontaneity of their riot or prison break.

Transportation/Consolidation Phase

This is also situation dependent. In some cases, the hostage takers have enough freedom to transport their victim(s) to a site they deem adequate as a confinement area. In other cases, the hostage takers are forced or choose to make do with what they have and remain at or near the capture site, setting up a defensive perimeter. In other words, a terrorist group may ambush a dignitary, throw him into a car, and transport him to a hideout. Or, a criminal may take over a liquor store and remain there with whatever customers and clerks he was able to take hostage — holding

Transport

Consolidation

out against the authorities outside the premises. He consolidates his position so that he is less vulnerable to the police surrounding the outside of the building.

Holding Phase

After the hostage is either moved to a holding location or after the captors have consolidated their position, the incident enters what is its most lengthy phase — holding. In many ways, this

Holding

is the safest phase for the hostage. The situation has had a chance to stabilize. There is little or no direct action taken by the authorities. Finally, a psychological phenomenon called the "Stockholm syndrome" (see Chapter Three) has an opportunity to develop. The Holding Phase is a waiting period and is filled with negotiations.

Termination Phase

Regardless of how a hostage-taking incident ends, the Termination Phase is generally a very tense time for all people involved in the crisis. The easiest and safest termination for the hostage is the voluntary release followed by a hostage taker's surrender. More dangerous is the escape, and most dangerous are the rescue by an outside force and the killing of the hostages as a means to end the crisis.

Termination

Hostage-Taking Locations

Are there any particular places that are more prone to hostage taking than others? The home and the office are common locations for kidnapping incidents — both criminal and terrorist, as well as domestic oriented incidents.

Liquor stores, convenience stores, fast-food restaurants, and banks are extremely common criminal hostage-taking locations.

Public transportation such as busses, trains, and airplanes are common for those hostage takers who wish to be transported from one place to another. Vehicles, such as automobiles, are common to terrorists, kidnappers, and escaping prisoners. Planes, as mentioned, are special in their notoriety, especially since 9/11.

Skyjacking

[2] "In a skyjacking, the first aim of the terrorists is to cause panic among the passengers in order for a few people (the terrorists) to be able to exercise absolute control over a large number of people (passengers and crew) in a confined space. While waiting to make their move, the hijackers have been building up to an emotional peak. At the moment they announce the hijack, they will usually make a lot of noise, show their weapons, and try to

Japanese Red Army Sky-Jack

create an appearance of chaos that only they can control. Submerging people in chaos guarantees the freezing of their reactions. The terrorists want to create the maximum amount of anxiety — fear of the unknown- in the minimum amount of time. The result is control by fear.

It is at the beginning of a flight that the hijackers are most primed. They are at their emotional peak. They must make their move soon in order to take advantage of a fully fueled aircraft that increases their alternatives for diverting and re-diverting the plane if that becomes necessary as landing rights are refused.

At the same time that the terrorists are at their emotional peak, the passengers are relaxed, glad to be on their way. Thus the terrorists and the passengers are at opposite ends of their emotional cycle, one peaking — one relaxing. That makes it so much easier to create the panic that leads to control."

Carjackings

Criminals will carjack for a variety of reasons — they need a vehicle to use in another robbery or a drive-by shooting; they want to take a joy ride; they're escaping another crime scene; to rob or rape the victims; or they want to sell the car and its parts.

[3] The statistics are against you — carjackers take on lone victims 92% of the time; 20% of the victims were injured; and 92% had weapons. The favorite carjacking locations are stop lights, parking lots, shopping centers, gas stations, car washes, convenience stores, and fast food drive-throughs.

Bob has done many trainings in Las Vegas. While out there, he was told carjackers like drive-throughs which have high curbs to the right of the lane to canalize the cars. The curbs make it much more difficult for the victim to escape.

What should you do to lessen the chances of getting carjacked? **Keep your doors locked and your windows shut!** The one thing found in common in incident after incident was the doors were unlocked and/or the windows were open, making it easier for the carjackers to enter the cars. **Don't allow the carjackers into your car!**

One morning Bob pulled into a parking slot at a convenience store. He went in, made his purchase, and returned to his car. As he entered his car, a women with two young children in carseats in the back pulled up alongside Bob. She left her keys in the car, the engine running, and the doors unlocked. Bob stayed where he was to watch over her vehicle and her little ones. She came back shortly and he chided her gently about leaving her children unprotected in a running car. She frowned, muttered under her breath, and drove off. People can be incredibly stupid at times.

Early one hot, Sunday morning a number of years ago in Leavenworth, Kansas, a man pulled into the parking lot of a grocery store. He exited the car, leaving its windows open. When he returned from the store, he got in, shut the door, and started the car. Suddenly he froze as two young men sat up in the back seat, one putting a gun to the man's head. They forced him to drive to Wyandotte lake twenty miles down the road, and had him park near their getaway car. It was determined these two had carjacked him as part of a pre-planned gang initiation. One of the youths sprayed charcoal lighter fluid all over the man and the interior of his car. The young men got out and tossed a lit match into the car, setting the man and his vehicle on fire. They quickly drove away and he jumped out of the car and dove into the lake to extinguish the flames. He then hid amongst a patch of cattail reeds for a couple of hours. Finally working up the courage to leave the lake, he managed to hitch hike to a hospital for burn treatment and to report to the authorities. This man should never have left his car open and he should have checked in back before getting in.

One important consideration is what to do if there are children in the car being carjacked. There was a very high profile case of a young mother who was carjacked in the Kansas City area. As her six-year-old boy tried to exit the car, the criminal took off, dragging the young boy who was caught in the seat belt. The carjacker drove for several miles at a high rate of speed with several passerbys giving chase. When they got him stopped, it was too late. The young boy had been drug to death.

This is not an easy decision, but if you love your children, stay with the vehicle until they are released. Carjackers have been known to toss infants in their carseats out of the windows or doors of moving vehicles into the street. Try to safeguard them as best you can.

Other Common Sites

Public streets are common for criminal hostage situations

since they are contiguous to common robbery sites. They are also popular for terrorists and kidnappers. Parking lots are especially dangerous for rape-kidnap incidents.

Public buildings such as airline and bus terminals and train stations are hijacker related danger zones. Courtrooms are dangerous because of attempted prisoner escapes. Prisons and jails are prone to riot and prison escape situations.

In other words, there are few truly safe areas free from the threat of hostage taking. As we review the above list of possible hostage-taking locations, it is apparent that safety is more a state of mind than it is a location. Another outstanding point is you don't have to be singled out as a prime terrorist victim to be at risk. Anybody in the wrong place at the wrong time may find himself in a hostage situation.

If we are all vulnerable to any of the various types of hostage situations, we should learn what to expect in these incidents. Let's examine the psychological environment of hostage situations so that we can learn how to safely and sanely function within them.

[1] *Random House College Dictionary*, Revised Edition, 1982, P. 640.

[2] Gayle Rivers, *The War Against the Terrorists: How to Win It*, Stein and Doubleday Publishers, 1986, P. 60.

[3] Chris E. McGoey, "Carjacking", http://www.crimedoctor.com/carjacking.htm, 2002

CHAPTER 3

EMOTIONAL / PSYCHOLOGICAL EXPECTATIONS

If you're ever so unfortunate to find yourself in the middle of a hostage situation, you'll need to be aware of the specific emotions and feelings you're liable to have at different times during the incident. You'll also need to understand what the hostage takers, negotiators, and possible rescuers are thinking and feeling.

By understanding the various psychological attitudes and motivations of the involved parties, you will be able to control your own emotions, to think objectively with a clear mind, and to use the interplay of all these emotions to your own advantage.

Hostage Feelings

When the incident begins, regardless of the type of hostage situation, the first emotion you are likely to feel is utter disbelief. "This couldn't be happening to me!" you'll think. This disbelief is a psychological coping mechanism known as denial — denying that the incident is real of which you are playing a part. You may be convinced that you're in no danger. [1] "This defense is common and effective but cannot be maintained for long. When denial does fade, the hostage has to face the danger to his life."

As soon as denial starts to fade, mind and body-numbing fear begins. Often a hostage will feel so powerless, shocked, and frightened that a temporary paralysis sets in. As we will mention in later chapters, escape attempts at this point will not likely be successful. The time for an early escape may only last the first ten seconds of the incident, before the hostage takers are completely in control. Once the incident is firmly underway, it is better to wait for a safer psychological and physical environment.

When this stage is reached, expect to feel helplessness and hopelessness, and disorientation. Often thoughts of escaping happen during this period but the hostage can't make his body or mind cooperate. Don't attempt an escape during this phase! The likelihood of a fatal hesitation is too great. WAIT!

One of the stranger common occurrences in hostage situations is a regression by the hostage to his childhood.
[2] "... being in a hostile environment, being isolated, and being helpless causes the hostage to forget past adult experiences and to resort to early adaptive behavior patterns from childhood." One female hostage found herself weeping constantly during an incident because she always got what she wanted from "Daddy" by crying nonstop.

The Stockholm Syndrome

This regression to childhood sets the stage for another common phenomenon known as the "Stockholm syndrome", so named after a bank robbery hostage situation in Sweden during the summer of 1973. 3 Jan-Erik Olsson, a professional safecracker and thief, recently escaped from prison, walked into the Sveriges Kreditbank of Stockholm brandishing a submachine gun. In the next six days, Olsson managed by means of the three women and one male hostage he was keeping, to hold the police at bay and to obtain the release of a former prison mate, Clark Olofsson. He eventually walked out in surrender with his hostages voluntarily clustered around him to protect him from police snipers.

The hostages had come to identify with their captor in a positive manner. One of the women even wanted to marry him. On the other hand, they were angry with the authorities for prolonging their captivity and not giving in to all of Olsson's demands for safe conduct to freedom.

[4] The syndrome has three components:

- Positive feelings on the part of the hostage toward the hostage taker.
- Negative feelings on the part of the hostage toward the authorities and rescuers.
- Positive feelings on the part of the hostage takers to ward the hostages.

[5] The regression to childhood feelings and actions by the hostage to the hostage taker sets up a striking similarity between the relationship of the hostage taker and that between an abused child and an abusive parent. The child clings to the abusive parent just as the hostage clings to the hostage taker. The abused child and the hostage with the Stockholm syndrome are strikingly similar in that both are loyal to the "parent" out of fear. Both feel threatened by intervening authorities and have a tendency to defend a cruel "parent". The gun of the hostage taker becomes the instrument that demands loyalty.

Hostage fear and anger toward authorities and rescuers are the result of concerns that their actions may cause the hostage taker to become violent, taking out his anger on the hostages. These negative feelings are exacerbated by the concern that the negotiator is stalling, thereby prolonging the unpleasantness of the incident. It is not uncommon for hostages to become more afraid of the police than they are of the abductors.

If you find yourself straining to "understand" your captor's viewpoint and striving to agree with it, you are experiencing Stockholm syndrome. Be aware of its development because you can expect the hostage taker to possibly reciprocate. There's a feeling of "we're all in this together".

It is not unusual to see the beginnings of this phenomenon after the first hour or so. Showing pictures of your family may help coax the abductor to see you as a fellow human as opposed to a faceless victim. You'll want to keep the incident as human as possible. It is when a hostage taker puts a bag over a hostage's head and face to make him seem less human, that the possibility death is increased. Its harder for a hostage taker to kill or harm someone they have started to identify with.

The hostage incidents in which the Stockholm syndrome has not been a factor have usually involved constant abuse from the hostage takers. Violent prison riots are generally just such situations. Where constant threat of life and torture are involved (very common in prison riots), there will seldom be a development of Stockholm syndrome.

In your anxiety, you may find yourself angered by any actions made by your fellow hostages which may disturb your captor. This is valid from the perspective that you don't want the boat rocked if it is going to endanger your safety. Also it's easier and safer to transfer your anger at being held onto a fellow hostage than it is to express anger toward your captor.

Typical Stockholm Syndrome Reaction

Hallucinations

You may find yourself experiencing unusual feelings and visions brought on by the stress of a hostage situation. If you have been isolated, confined, restrained of movement, and subjected to life-threatening danger, you may experience hallucinations and claustrophobia. [6] A study of various types of hostage victims was conducted by Dr. Ronald K. Siegal of the University of California's School of Medicine. These included rape, robbery, terrorist, kidnap, POW, and UFO hostages. Out of the thirty one subjects, eight reported having hallucinations. Each category of hostage produced hallucinations so we know the phenomenon doesn't depend on

Hallucinating

who takes you captive. The consistent factor was the combination of conditions mentioned above. If you are kept tied up in a small, dark room or closet by yourself and are threatened with death by your captor, you may have one or more of the following unusual experiences:

- Sensitivity of your eyes to light and difficulty in focusing your eyes.
- Flashes of light and geometric forms.
- Sensations of being in a tunnel, hallway, elevator, dark alley, corridor, or funnel.
- Detachment from what's going on — out-of-body expe riences.
- Childhood and other past experiences relived in great detail.
- Voices and other auditory distortions.

Your mind is accustomed to constant stimulation. When your mind is deprived of its stimulation, it will manufacture its own. This does not mean you are going crazy, it only means that your mind is coping with a bad situation. Once you are released, you may have flashbacks. Understand them for what they are- harmless perceptual accommodations. In Chapter Four we will give you a number of useful techniques that will help you cope with inactivity and confinement. These helpful techniques may allow you to stave off problems with hallucinations and claustrophobia.

The Hostage Takers

At the start of a hostage incident, the hostage taker is at his most dangerous state of mind. He too is frightened- afraid of the consequences of failure, afraid of being hurt or dying, afraid of losing his freedom, and afraid of losing control. His nerves are on a hair trigger. You may scratch an itch and find yourself getting shot for your movement which he interpreted as threatening. Keep your eyes averted. Do not challenge him or argue or question his commands in any way at this point. Later on, when the Stockholm syndrome has had a chance to develop, you may try some of these things. By that time, he will have calmed down a little and should be more reasonable. The most important things for him at the beginning of the incident is to assure his own safety and to gain complete control of the situation as quickly as possible. Those people who try to thwart him in any way or just appear to do so in his eyes, put themselves and others at great risk. Hang tight for the moment!

You should understand that not all hostage takers are alike. Some are less dangerous than others. [7] "The hostage taker who is a genuine political terrorist is unlikely to be capricious or irrational. He is also unlikely to be affected by appeals to personal selfish interests: that is, he cannot usually be bought off. He is conscious of the high risks he takes in his exploits, but does not protect himself from danger in the way that either a criminal or a policeman would. Yet for all that, he is a professional. He is dedicated to his job and, though he may want very much to avoid dying, he knows that he may have to."

The professional criminal, on the other hand (with the exception of kidnappers), will normally only take hostages as a last ditch effort to stay free. Given time to think about his alternatives, he'll give himself up rather than harm the hostages and earn an even longer prison term. A kidnapper, however, is very dangerous. Once he has gotten you to confirm that he has you and that you are still well, your value decreases. Many kidnappers kill their victims to prevent later identification. Terrorists, on the other hand, want media attention and usually don't mind being identified.

Carjackers, for the most part, are violent thugs. They don't care about you or your family. They'll do whatever they have to do to get your car and get away.

Another dangerous hostage taker is the prison convict, especially murderers doing life equivalent sentences (99 years with no parole) or death-row time. They may escape, taking hostages once they are clear of the prison, or they may take part in a prison riot and have access to prison administration hostages. These people have nothing to lose. Within prison walls, murder is a common occurrence.

One night Bob was teaching a Business Law college class to prisoner students in the US Penitentiary, Leavenworth, Kansas. Suddenly the guards rushed into the classroom and herded all the students out and back to their cell blocks. When asked by a guard if he was all right, Bob said yes and asked why all the concern. The guard said, "Because, we just found a blood-trail in this wing of the prison. We thought it might be yours."

A short time later they found a frightened prisoner hiding at the end of a hallway. He had a badly lacerated hand and claimed he had fallen and cut it on the stairs. The guard lieutenant said later that he had probably been "shanked" (stabbed by a makeshift weapon made from dining hall cutlery) and had caught or blocked it with his hand and then ran away.

Life has little value in prison. Often someone's life is worth the price of two cartons of cigarettes or a week of free sex from someone's personal homosexual lover. These murders, or "hits", are generally committed by a prisoner with nothing left to lose. The Lieutenant told a story of how he had come upon a hit man in the act of shanking another prisoner. The Lieutenant yelled, "Put the shank down!"

The hit man said, "You want me to put the shank down, motherf...er? I'll put the shank down!" and he did — right into the chest of the victim who, by this time, had collapsed on the floor with a total of twenty-seven stab wounds.

You see, the hit man had nothing to lose except for some time in solitary confinement, which he knew he had to serve in any case, now that he had been caught. Thus, he fulfilled his contract and would maintain a macho, stand-up reputation.

Another story illustrating how cheap life is in prison: Bob was teaching management classes to military convicts serving time in the Ft. Leavenworth Military Disciplinary Barracks. During break time one night, a guard told the story of how one of the prisoners had arrived at the gates fighting his guards. He proceeded to get into fights with fellow prisoners and guards on a regular basis. Although he was thrown into the "hole" as punishment, he continued to be a problem prisoner. After several tries at rehabilitation, the administration exercised a well-established option and transferred him two miles down the road to the Federal Penitentiary. Within two weeks of his transfer, he was found murdered. He had made the mistake of disturbing the old-timer Federal convicts. Rather than put up with his nonsense, they terminated the problem.

If you are taken hostage by a prisoner, be extremely careful! Some will kill with little or no provocation. These people have only contempt for "civilians" and are totally self-oriented. The only things that matter to them are their own needs and feelings, no one elses'.

The last type of hostage taker is the emotionally disturbed or insane person. This may be an irate father trying to take custody of his kids from his estranged wife, it may be a jilted lover seeking revenge, or a truly insane person. According to FBI Special Agent Thomas Strentz:

[8] "Recent research has identified five types of hostage takers in the United States (Strentz, 1984): two types suffer from personality disorders, the antisocial and the inadequate, two types suffer from psychotic disorders — depression and paranoid schizophrenic, and one type is motivated by political-religious ideology."

The first two, the antisocial and the inadequate, have a hard time coping with day-to-day life, such as family or work related problems. They need to feel powerful, never challenge them!

The greatest number of hostage situations in the United States are caused by disturbed people like those who have a complaint or a score to settle and take hostages to force the authorities into giving them "Justice".

Emotional/Psychological Expectations

Of all those mentioned above, the most dangerous are the paranoid schizophrenics. These people are not in touch with the same reality which normal people experience. They have delusions, hear voices and see visions no one else can hear or see. They may think they are better than anyone else (delusions of grandeur) or they may believe that someone or everyone is out to get them. They usually want attention, recognition, and/or satisfaction. They may also want material things like a car or money. They trust no one, making it extremely difficult to negotiate with them.

They have very sensitive feelings about sexual dysfunctions and their sexual identity. These people are very volatile and unpredictable. The paranoid schizophrenic tends to project his own feelings of self hate and self anger onto others. A typical logical train of thought for this person would be, "I don't hate me, **you** hate me and are causing me to suffer!" They read into typical life events meanings totally different from the norm. You cannot reason with them and anything could excite or irritate them. They are prone to high levels of anger and violence.

Students, as well as workers, may well fit into this category. The two young men who shot up the Columbine high school had been made into pariahs by their fellow students. They coldheartedly
decided to obtain revenge while going out in a blaze of glory. [9] There are many other factors besides peer harassment which can cause students to flip out — a bad family life, poor conflict resolution skills, negative self-images, and many others, including an administration's failure to recognize warning signs.

Negotiators/Authority Figures

The authorities and their negotiators are often considered to be the real targets or victims of a hostage situation. This may not make sense to a terrified hostage; however, in the larger scheme of the Universe it makes sense. In every kind of hostage situation, except for a kidnapping, it is the authorities from which the hostage takers seek to extract favors and not the hostage. Alas, the hostage is a captive audience. It is the authority power structure that stands to lose the respect and confidence of the population base which it protects. It must also protect the hostages' lives. To do so, they must negotiate, trying to stretch out the time so that the hostage takers become worn out and finally give up the hostages safely. Although lengthening the situation helps to defuse it in many cases, it is rather hard on the hostages. This is one of the reasons why the Stockholm syndrome develops the way that it does. The hostages perceive the negotiators' stall tactics and believe that they are purposely trying to prolong and increase the danger.

The poor negotiator gets it from all sides. He's under pressure from his superiors to end the situation safely and with the power structure still in control. He's under pressure from the hostage takers to accede to their demands, and he's under pressure from the hostages to give away anything and everything that will end the situation as quickly as possible. He has to balance these conflicting agendas while trying to maintain a calm, positive attitude. His is an unenviable position. Remember, he really is trying to work toward your safe release; however, he must do so on his own timetable.

Rescuers

Hostage rescue is one of the toughest soldiering jobs there is. We say "soldier" because a rescue take-down is military (or at least paramilitary) in nature. Whether the rescue team is a police SWAT team or an elite military Commando force, all within it train together as one unit. Many hours of practice are spent training for contingencies such as a hostage situation. Its members are cohesive, that is, they understand one another and have similar goals. They work well together. They are talented professionals with one goal in mind — to save the hostages. Normally they are not sent in unless the negotiations have broken down or because the hostages are in imminent danger.

Before they enter the confinement area, they will probably have experienced long hours of interminable waiting. They have had to keep themselves ready to go at all times without knowing if or when their services would be required.

Once they have been ordered in, the assault may seem almost like a release. It has been said that war is a series of long periods of boredom punctuated by short moments of sheer terror. Hostage rescuers lead a similar existence.

When they come in, it will be fast and forceful. At this moment, they may experience the normal fear of combat; however, their training will allow them to sublimate this while they concentrate on finding and recognizing the hostage takers, neutralizing them as quickly as possible, and immediately clearing everyone out of the confinement area. Don't expect them to be overly solicitous at this point. They will probably be acting like well-oiled machinery without much emotion of any kind other than abruptness. Once the takedown is over; however, they should start loosening up.

The high degree of concentration required to separate friends from foes and to shoot with consistent, deadly accuracy leaves little room for any emotional involvement.

Flow State

During the takedown, both the hostages and the rescuers may experience what martial artists call the Flow State. During extremely violent action, one may notice that time has slowed down. Everything looks as if it is happening in slow motion. This lends an air of detachment and unreality to what is taking place. This is a common occurrence in combat situations. Don't worry about it or try to fight it. Flow State is a survival reaction and is very useful. It is the result of your reaction reflexes and your perceptual acuity speeding up. This state will quickly pass. It merely means your mind and body are working together for a short while at maximum efficiency.

Conclusions

Hostage situations produce high stress states in all involved participants. As a hostage, you should learn what emotional states you will experience. Learn to recognize your transference of fear and anger onto others and try to control it. Try not to let the feelings of helplessness grind you down. Constantly seek to work through you emotions. Remain submissive and watch for the Stockholm syndrome to start working for you as the hostage taker begins to feel sorry for you. Remain patient with the authorities' negotiator. Remember, he is working for you. Try to stay down and calm during the rescue attempt and let the professional rescuers do their job. Above all else, try to keep your perspective!

[1] Cassie L. Wesselius, M.D., LCDR MC USNR, and James V. Sarno, FBI Special Agent; "The Anatomy of a Hostage Situation"; *Behavioral Sciences & The Law*, Vol. 1, No. 2,1983, P. 44.

[2] Ibid.

[3] Jan Schreiber, *The Ultimate Weapon*, William Morrow and Company, Inc., 1978, P. 43-45.

[4] Wesselius and Sarno, P.44.

[5] Ibid. P. 43.

[6] Ronald K. Siegal, PhD, "Hostage Hallucinations: Visual Imagery Induced by Isolation and Life-Threatening Stress", *The Journal of Nervous and Mental Disease*, 1984, P. 264-276.

[7] Schreiber, P. 99.

[8] Thomas Strentz, "Negotiating with the Hostage-Taker Exhibiting Paranoid Schizophrenic Symptoms", *Journal of Police Science and Administration*, Vol 14, No. 1, 1986, P. 12.

[9] Kramen, Massey, and Timm, *Preventing and Responding to School Violence*, International Assoc of Chiefs of Police, 1999, P. 2.

CHAPTER 4

COPING WITH CAPTIVITY

Disorientation

Hostage takers often will attempt to keep their captives in a disoriented state to make them more tractable. You may find that your watch and any pocket calendars you have on you are taken away. This is done to help you lose track of time. You may be kept incommunicado from other captives. You may be kept bound or shackled, possibly blindfolded in dark, cramped quarters. Again, this is done to keep you docile and off-balance. To combat this, you should try to create your own internal clock based upon activities going on around you, such as how often your guard is changed or how often you are fed. Listen to any sounds coming from outside your area of confinement to cue upon such as traffic or farm animal sounds. Listen for repetition patterns and cyclical occurrences. Try to use anything that will give you an indication of the passage of time.

Once you have determined the equivalent of a day in your life, try to keep track of those days by making marks or scratches on a makeshift calendar.

Keep Prepared

Studies of prisoners of war indicate that those who survived shared some common attributes. If a high-risk job places you in situations that are fraught with hostage taking danger, you might want to consider these points and acquire them for your own:

- Good physical health prior to capture.
- A rich, full, satisfying life.
- A strong self-identity or sense of self.
- Purpose and meaning in life — a sense of values and objectives.
- Success and achievement.

Making the Time Count

Experienced criminals have told us that whenever a wise prisoner was locked away in solitary confinement for a long time, he would use the time to exercise his body and his mind. In that way, a negative, boring punishment was turned into a positive experience. The same holds true for hostages. Captivity is boring and wears one down over time. Boredom can increase feelings of helplessness in a hostage. These feelings can in turn engender long-term adverse psychological impacts. There have been numerous findings from prisoner of war experiences and the yearlong American Embassy Iranian Hostage situation that support this premise.

The purpose of this chapter is to provide examples and specific techniques that will help relieve the boredom of captivity and can be used to enhance your daily life as well.

Physical Activity

Lets first look at what can be done to keep one physically healthy and alert. This is extremely important if you hope to make an escape from long-term captivity where you are more likely to become rundown and out of shape. When its time to make a break for freedom, you must be physically capable of fighting, climbing, running, and walking.

Many of the American Embassy hostages in Iran maintained regular exercise routines. [1] Two of the women, Miss Elizabeth Ann Smith and Miss Kathryn Koob, exercised three times a day: from noon until 1:00 PM, at 5:30 PM for 45 minutes, and at 10:30 PM they would exercise 45 minutes more, running figure-eights or circles around their room.

[2] Colonel Schaefer exercised twice a day, once at noontime for an hour or so of yoga and walking around his room, then more of the same for an hour at night.

Some of the hostages were fanatical about their exercise. Marine Sgt. Gregory Persinger recalled, [3] "I would wake up at 10 in the morning, walk an hour, exercise for close to 2 1/2 hours doing 1,000 sit-ups to begin with, push-ups and regular calisthenics. After that, I would sit up and read maybe, a couple of hours until the food came for lunch. Then more walking, more exercise, more reading, and finally to bed."

[4] Richard Morefield said he had been overweight — 210 pounds when he was captured. He exercised, touching his toes and performing other simple routines when his captivity began, then gradually increasing the program until, by the end of his captivity, he was doing 50 off-the-wall push-ups, numerous squat jumps and sit-ups and an hour's jogging in his room. He weighed 178 pounds when he reached Wiesbaden.

You may find yourself in a hostage situation which does not allow you much freedom to physically exercise for long periods of time. Your captors might keep you chained to a radiator in a Beirut apartment; however, you can still get some exercise by using the following methods:

Isometric Exercises will allow you to maintain a minimum of muscle tone. Isometrics involve working two opposing muscle groups against one another in a static position. For example, try to do a curl with one arm while the other holds it and prevents it from moving through the curl motion. The disadvantage of isometrics is that since the limb does not move through its full range of motion, it becomes weaker when passing through those positions not exercised.

Dynamic Tension Exercises are considered to be a better approach to exercise than Isometrics. These are similar in that one muscle group applies resistance to another's movement; however, the entire range of motion is allowed. For example, Resist the curl movement as before, except this time allow enough motion for the arm to complete the movement with steady resistance to it all the way.

The static stretches of Yoga are excellent to maintain and even increase muscle and tendon tone, flexibility, and elasticity

Isometric Curl

Dynamic Tension Curl

A Yoga Stretch

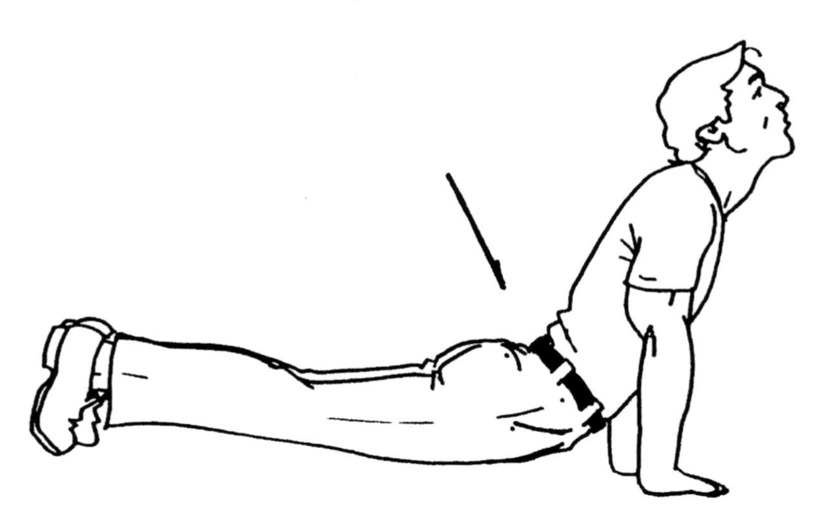

throughout your body.

In any case, doing some type of physical exercise is better than doing nothing at all. Your lymphatic system is responsible for carrying waste products (toxins) away from your body's cells. It can only do this important job when your muscles move and contract. That is why animals and small children instinctively stretch immediately upon awakening from sleep. They do this to remove toxins that have collected during the relatively inactive slumber period. This is also why many people feel so awful when they sleep too long. It's really important to do something physical for your health's sake and to relieve boredom.

Maintaining Health

If you require any medicines on a regular basis or if you have any medical conditions that require regular attention or treatment, be sure to let your captors know. They have a vested interest in keeping you healthy for either propaganda purposes, if they are terrorists, or for their own security, if they are criminals.

Mental Activity

Just as it is important to be active physically, it is also very important to keep mentally active. Ask for reading and writing materials, it's worth a try anyway. If they won't give them to you, you will have to fall back on your own resources. Many of our prisoners of war in the hands of the Vietnamese communists used a variety of mental techniques to relieve boredom and to keep mentally active.

One man built his dream house in his mind — brick by brick, nail by nail, board by board. Others played games such as chess or bridge in their heads. The more fortunate American Embassy hostages had real games and books to keep them occupied.

The importance of certain kinds of mental activity cannot be overstressed, especially meditation and deep contemplation. It can be religious or secular in nature. In September, 1988, Bob presented a paper at the 1988 Seoul Olympic Scientific Congress in Korea. During the Congress he had the good fortune to meet Sports Psychologist, Kurt Krueger, Founder and Director of the Institute of Sports Psychology in West Los Angeles. When Bob mentioned this book as one of his latest projects, Kurt said, "I was once hijacked by the Japanese Red Army and meditation pulled me through it safely. It even earned me an early release."

Bob was excited by this news since he was looking for specific examples of meditation usage in hostage situations. Kurt had been an All-American swimmer and a coach of world record holders. This was no whimpy, half-starved aesthetic, but a vigorous, physical man extolling the virtues of mental exercise during hostage situations. Bob asked him about his experience and Kurt told him the following story of how deep religious contemplations and meditation pulled him through a harrowing experience.

In the fall of 1977, Kurt had been living in Ganeshpuri, India, studying Yoga in a Hindu Ashram (a communal religious school). Having recently decided to return to a teaching position in Los Angeles, he traveled to Bombay to connect with a flight back to the US. Here is his fascinating story:

"I got to the airport at 3:30 the next morning, and the plane took off about 7:00. About an hour after takeoff, when I was just beginning to wonder about breakfast, the whole thing began. There was some yelling in the back of the plane, and then several men wearing business suits and carrying guns ran down the aisle past me, yelling and screaming, and headed for the front of the plane.

I said, 'Okay, God, here we go.' It was obvious to me that the plane was being hijacked, and it was also obvious to me that I couldn't do anything about it and that God was going to have to handle the whole situation. I remembered what my wife had said.

'If you get into any difficulty, just turn to God. He'll take care of things.' I happened to have in my flight bag a medicine bottle full of Holy water. I took a sip of it, and sat back and repeated a mantra (a word repeated over and over to improve concentration).

It was an intense time on the plane. A baby started crying the moment the yelling started and everybody was very nervous because nobody was sure what was going to happen. I picked up a religious book, but before I could open it, one of the men returned to our compartment wielding a .38 automatic pistol and a hand grenade.

He said, 'Fasten your seat belts. Put your hands behind your head. Don't talk. Don't look at me.' I did manage, however, to get a few glances in. He was short, well built and impeccably dressed in a conservative pin-striped suit and tie. He seemed to be about my age- late twenties or early thirties. From his features he was obviously Japanese.

The hijacker seemed to be as nervous as the passengers. But there was one big difference: he was in command. Oddly enough, I felt no antagonism toward him, and just as oddly, I didn't feel any coming from him toward me. I had a sense that we were in this drama together, he playing his part and me playing mine.

After about forty-five minutes later, my arms began to ache. I told the hijacker my arms were falling asleep in that position and asked him if we could put our hands down. He said, 'No.' He wasn't going to budge an inch from his demands.

A few minutes later, though, he did let us put our hands down, when he announced that we should turn over our passports, our watches, and any pins or weapons we happened to be carrying. A man sitting several rows in front of me stood up and reached into the luggage compartment over his head. The hijacker was beside him in an instant and clipped him on the side of the face with his gun. 'Obey orders, obey orders, obey orders!', the hijacker commanded. Then the man told him that he had been obeying orders, and that he had been trying to get his passport out of his jacket pocket, and the hijacker immediately apologized for hitting him.

A few minutes later, a man whispered something to a person sitting next to him and the hijacker walked over to him and gave him the same glancing blow on the side of his head.

These were dramatic little scenes, which some of the passengers later described as vicious and unprovoked. But what struck me most about those moments was that the hijacker didn't seem malicious. I didn't have the feeling that he wanted to hurt anyone. He was just playing out his role of hijacker, just doing what he felt was necessary at the time. And, in fact, it was effective. People didn't talk or move from their seats after that.

Within the next few minutes, the hijackers efficiently collected our hand luggage and bags. When they said, 'You can keep your money, medicine, and jewelry' — I removed the water bottle and quickly took another sip. Then I began to read a passage from my religious book. I read it with intense concentration, seven or eight times from the beginning to the end. I said the words of this passage over and over all the way to Dacca, Bangladesh, which is where the hijackers decided to land.

Shortly before the plane landed in Dacca, one of the hijackers asked me to put the book down. Once I stopped reading about the power of God, I realized that I was experiencing that power within me. During the entire time I had been reading, I had been fully absorbed, with no fear in my mind, no other thoughts. And then when I stopped, I felt totally at peace.

Although I was silently absorbed in the fruits of my hours of chanting during the landing, most of the other passengers were in an entirely different state. The baby who had started to cry when the hijackers first took over the plane started crying again, letting out wails of terror. And as I looked around the plane, it seemed to me that the baby was the only passenger free to vocalize what I could see manifested on almost every face on the plane. Many of the men had a tight, anxious look around their mouths, and some of the women were crying quietly.

I, on the other hand, felt almost ecstatic. Not that I found the situation pleasant. It was extremely unpleasant. But it didn't have the power to affect me in the same way that it did the other people.

While the plane was approaching the Dacca airport, I took another sip of water, and I turned to the man sitting next to me and said, 'This is my medicine. I have an enlarged heart.' I was, of course, making a private joke. What I didn't know at the time was that those words would come in handy later on, that they would be the key to getting me off the plane at the earliest possible moment.

Just before we landed in Dacca, the concentration of anxious energy in the plane was, by now, painfully intense. Even the hijackers seemed nervous. They had put their guns and hand grenades in their belts after the first hour or so, but for the landing they started waving the firearms around again, telling people not to move, not to talk. At some point in the morning they had covered their faces with the kind of loose masks that nomads wear in Middle Eastern deserts, and this just added to the whole atmosphere of anxiety.

The hijacker moved an elderly woman into the window seat next to mine. After a few minutes, she looked like she was going to collapse, and her hands began to shake wildly. I put my hand on hers and said quietly, 'Just calm down. Everything will be okay. The Lord is taking care of us.' And immediately, she relaxed.

At that point something unusual started happening to me. I began to breath irregularly. It was like nothing I had ever experienced before. It was so pronounced that after a short time the hijacker who was controlling the second class compartment took me up to the first class section. He plopped me on the floor there, and at that moment my body began to go into spasms, and I started to experience some pain in my chest, in the area of my heart.

While this was going on, I was completely calm, even unconcerned about what was happening to my body. I wasn't fearful because I knew that God was taking care of me. I was able to say, 'mmm.. .mmeehh...mmmeddd...meedddicine.' I had difficulty with my breath and my body was moving so violently that I felt drained of all energy. The hijackers went back to my seat and the man who had been sitting in the aisle seat next to me gave them my bottle of medicine', the water.

The hijackers brought the water up to me and poured a little in my mouth. I soon stopped breathing altogether. I must have stopped for quite some time because I could feel someone putting pressure on my chest, as if I were being given a closed heart massage. Then a large pill was stuffed under my tongue, and someone gave me a shot. I didn't know what they were giving me, and for a moment I felt some concern. I felt that what was happening to me had nothing to do with a heart attack, and it occurred to me that if I wasn't sick, the medicine they were giving me might make me sick. Then I thought, if God is taking care of all this, how could they possibly hurt me? So, I stopped worrying.

It was obvious to me that the whole episode was simply a gift from God. The pain that seemed to be associated with my physical heart was much more likely connected to an internal energy center in the vicinity of my heart. In fact there was every reason to believe that God was behind this episode and that it was not a physical heart attack that I was experiencing, that it was a yogic catharsis. I was thirty-one years old and in excellent health. I had been an athlete most of my life, sick for only about three days a year, and then with only minor illnesses. Besides, since I had been living in an Ashram for a year, I was hardly living the kind of life that was conducive to heart seizure.

One of the characteristics of Siddha Yoga is that once the inner energy is activated it works within to cleanse and purify the body. Through subtle inner processes, it removes all blocks and obstacles which prevent a person from experiencing the limitless love which lies within him and within all human beings. These purification processes can take many forms. Sometimes a serious meditator will begin to spontaneously do what I did on the plane; they experience rapid breathing or retention of breath.

Since I had often heard about and many times witnessed these purification processes, it occurred to me, as I lay on my back on the floor of that first class section of a commandeered DC-8, that this is what was happening to me. The only thing that could get me off that plane fast was the appearance of a serious illness. So it seemed to me that God had chosen this opportune time to work on my heart center. I could never have faked a heart attack on my own. I don't know what a heart attack looks like. I have never had one, and I've never even seen one. But there I was, watching my body go through the whole act faultlessly.

During this time, it became extremely hot on the plane. We had landed in midafternoon in the steaming tropics, and we weren't hooked up for any ventilation. I don't know what the temperature reading in the plane was, but it was so hot that if you put your hand on the side of the seat, you had to pull it away. It felt like a frying pan. The people who were standing over me were dripping sweat onto me, into my mouth and eyes. This compounded the discomfort of the pain in my chest. In fact, the heat became so intense that the men took off their clothes and were walking around in their underwear. The women stayed in their seats, absolutely soaking their clothes through with sweat. It was so hot that the oxygen masks above the seats were automatically released. After a few hours of this suffocating heat, one man began to crack up. He began to scream, 'I would rather die than live like this! Let me out of here. Kill me now and get it over with!' The hijackers calmed the man down by telling him that the airport officials had granted two of their demands, one for air-conditioning and the other for water.

So, after about five hours of post-landing heat, the air-conditioning was finally hooked up and some water was brought on board. The temperature dropped to normal and kept on going down. In no time everybody started to freeze. By then it was late afternoon, and my body was still having spasms. But as night came, my body calmed down some, and the hijackers finally gave me some food: a dinner roll, two small crackers, and a piece of cheese about the size of one of the crackers. That was all the food that any of the passengers got during the twenty-seven hours that I was on the plane.

Once my body stopped having spasms and I could talk more easily, I asked the hijackers about letting me off the plane so that I could go to a hospital. They didn't reply one way or the other, and I began to feel a little impatient with them. So I lay back and worked at a mantra, repeated it, listened to it, and let everything else fall away in the background.

I knew that God was in control of this whole play, and I had to let everything happen in his time, not mine. Here I had experienced all these physical movements which were the perfect way for me to get off the plane, and I knew that soon enough, when the moment was right, I was going to be released. So once again I released my worries to God.

I got sporadic rest on the floor that night, and the passenger who was lying on the seat above me, a former California assemblyman, kept describing the hijackers and their weapons to me, so that if I did get off the plane early, I could give some solid information to the authorities. All around us, people in the first class compartment were resting the way we were: one person on the seat, another on the floor beneath. In second class, it was much more crowded, of course, and people were cramped into their seats, lying in the aisles, and generally stretching out in any way they could. Everywhere people were experiencing a great deal of discomfort throughout the night.

When the morning came, one of the hijackers stopped at my seat and lifted me up. 'Where are we going?' I asked him.

'Our demands have been met, ' he said. 'We're letting you off the plane.'

He took me to the cockpit, and there I was given something like a briefing by a man I assumed was the head hijacker, as he seemed to have been giving most of the orders during the flight. The man told me that I was headed for Tokyo, and he said when I got there I would see big city bustling with people. He said what I would not see is the fear and oppression that underlie this scene. He said that he and the other hijackers were trying to free political prisoners, and then he apologized for what had happened to me.

The hijackers threatened to blow up the plane and everyone on it. They were asking, I found out later, for the release of nine political prisoners in Japan and six million dollars in ransom in exchange for the hostages on board the plane. They ended up getting all of the money and six of the people they asked for. (Three of the prisoners refused to come with them.)

After a short while, the hijackers let five of us off the plane: myself, the assemblyman's wife, who was pregnant; and the family with the child who cried so piercingly during the flight. The plane took off from the Dacca airport two and a half days later, landing first in Kuwait, then Syria, and finally Algeria, where it was reported that they paid the ransom money to the government in exchange for political asylum. The hijackers let the passengers off in groups at their different stops- the final three passengers, including the assemblyman, were released in Syria, on Sunday afternoon, five days after the whole drama had begun.

I had gotten off the plane at about noon on Thursday. Soon after I was released, I underwent a series of checkups with doctors, discussions with government and airport officials, and interviews with the army of reporters who followed the five of us around for the next several days. We spent a day and a half in Dacca, then flew, in stages, to Bangkok, Tokyo, and finally, Los Angeles.

The big question concerning my experiences on the plane was a medical one. Had I actually undergone a heart attack or had something else happened? The doctors in Dacca told me right after my release that my blood pressure was normal. The electrocardiogram, taken in Los Angeles about a week after the 'attack', was also normal. And my cholesterol count, when it was checked later on, proved to be below normal. The doctor who examined me in Los Angeles said, You could have had a heart attack.' But both she and I doubted it.

What really happened on that plane, as far as I was concerned, is that God enabled me to experience the good and bad fortunes, the comforts and discomforts of the physical body in a detached way, as though my body were something apart from me. What happened on the plane is that I experienced this detachment, so that it wasn't just something I had read about in books on yoga and philosophy, it was something that I knew. Unless you actually experience something, it's just another little mind game. It may sound good to your mind, but it isn't really a part of you. It isn't full, it isn't complete."

Kurt Krueger is unusual in that he was a highly experienced meditator and had just come off an intensive year of developing inner strength and enhancing the use of his body's energies. The nice thing about mental exercises, however, is that you don't have to be guru material to do them or to receive benefit from them. The following mental exercises will not only help eat up empty time, they are extremely healthy for you in several aspects. They come from Bob's extensive research into the martial arts and sports psychology. Some of them are used by world-class athletes to better physical performance in their respective areas of expertise.

Relaxation Response

All these mental exercises require a relaxed body. The following suggestions will allow you to relax quickly and will eventually train your body to slip automatically into a relaxed state. There are several approaches or procedures. All work but its best to mix their use from time to time to prevent boredom (the very thing you're trying to relieve). These methods require you to sit on a straight chair or lie on a bed or a floor.

Gently close your eyes, let your limbs hang or lie relaxed without crossing them. Let the tip of your tongue rest lightly against the roof of your mouth.

The first procedure is to think to yourself that your feet are heavy and relaxed and feeling good. As you think this, your feet really will feel heavy. Gradually work up your body through your ankles, calves, knees, thighs, hips, lower back, stomach, middle back, chest, fingers, hands, wrists, lower arms, upper arms, shoulders, neck, scalp, eyes, jaw, and finally your forehead. Your body should feel very heavy and relaxed by now.

The second procedure is the reverse, starting with your head and working down your body.

The third procedure is to think your body parts warm and relaxed from bottom to top.

The fourth procedure is the same as the third, but begin with your head and work down to your feet.

Visualizations

Once your body is relaxed, visualize in your mind's eye specific physical activities. Perhaps the most important type of activity is the act of escaping. Rehearse it over and over in great vi-

Visualizing Escape

sual detail within your mind. World Class athletes often do this. The great American diver, Greg Louganis, did this before every dive. That is one reason why his performances were usually so perfectly executed. He had practiced each dive thousands of times in his head. When it was time for him to do it in real life, it was old hat to him.

In Bob's Hapkido classes, the last fifteen minutes were usually spent going on complex "Head Trips" using visualization techniques. After relaxing his class, he talked them through scenarios that reinforced the training they received that day. In their minds' eyes, they found themselves floating up through the ceiling of the gym and down along paths in a nearby city forest. They may have been coached through threatening situations requiring them to use skills they learned that day, or they may have been talked through the feelings they would experience in actual combat so as not to be distracted by them when the time came to put their skills into use. Bob had some highly experienced martial art students who took his classes primarily for the effective mental conditioning training he provided.

Meditation Techniques

These next techniques not only kill time, they are wonderful for both your physical and emotional health. They are best done early upon rising and in the evening before dinner. They should never be done right after a meal. Some of these mental exercises may seem rather unusual; however, they work very well. Some of these are based upon Chinese medicine principles and Indian Yoga practices thousands of years old. Some are based upon martial art exercises developed during this century. If you do them with regularity, get ready for some mind-blowing positive experiences. Needless to say, you don't have to be a hostage to enjoy any of these techniques and procedures, practice them for your daily life. Have fun with your new head!

Breathing Meditations

These first techniques deal with breathing meditation. The center of gravity of your body and the center of its physical power is also the center of a mysterious life force called KI (key) or CHI (chee). This center lies about three inches below the navel and just inside your abdomen. The Chinese call it the Tan Tien, the Koreans call it the Tan Jun, the Japanese call it the Hara, and the East Indians call it the Hatha. Every major Oriental culture professes the existence of this point; therefore, this center of power is important to many breathing meditations which are designed to increase KI. So important is the concept of an internal energy force that one finds it as a portion of many martial art styles' names such as:

- Tai Chi Chuan
- Aikido
- Hapkido

Seat yourself comfortably in a straight chair or on a couple of pillows on the floor. Allow your back to stay straight upright. (See the illustration). Place the tip of your tongue on the roof of your mouth. Breath in through your nose for six heart beats and then breath out for six heart beats. In your mind's eye, imagine a flow of energy traveling up your spine to the top of your head as you breath in. As you breath out, imagine that same energy flowing down the front of your body (on the inside) to your Tan Tien. Once you have managed to do the 6/6 heart beats for a few minutes, try using 9/9 heart beats for awhile. Every few minutes add three more heart beats for each in and out breath until you work up to 30/30 heart beats. It may take several days or even weeks of practice until you can do the 30/30 slow breathing. Don't try to rush it. The more you do, the better this exercise becomes. Start out with 20-minute sessions and increase the length of the sessions as you feel comfortable.

This exercise is going to cause some unusual reactions in your body. When Bob first worked up to the 30/30 level, he found himself becoming drenched with sweat.

Breathing meditation tends to cleanse one's body and to generate and enhance KI power. It's a good idea not to do this exercise right before going to bed at night because it is too invigorating. Eventually you must learn to concentrate on the energy flow around the circle in your body rather than on the breath and try to feel its flow around your body.

To complete the meditation, keep your eyes closed and rub the palms of your hands together counterclockwise a few times until they are warm from friction. Place your warm palms over your closed eyes and breath in their warmth for three times, then lower your hands and open your eyes. Doing this exercise will allow you to begin sensing subtle changes in your body and will help your mind and body get in tune with one another. You will be amazed at how time distorts while doing breathing meditation.

The Grand Circle of KI

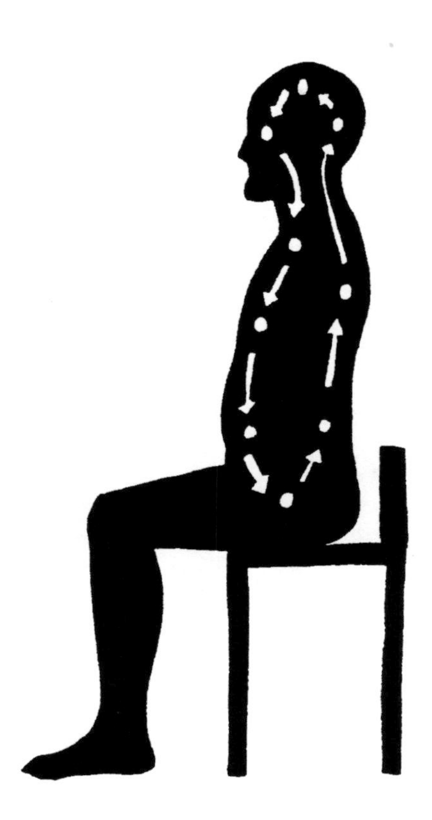

Color Breathing

At this point we will address some stranger and yet even more effective techniques. These come under a common heading of Color Breathing, which combines meditation with visualization techniques. There is nothing very magical about these procedures. They are based on the fact that certain visual cues can have effects on the body's physical sensations. Again, the purpose is to integrate the mind with the body in a positive manner so they work in harmony with one another. Its a well known fact that stress (and what could be more stressful than a hostage situation), can cause debilitating physical effects. Negative emotions of fear and anxiety can make us physically ill as our bodies react chemically to these cues. These next exercises can help counteract this phenomenon by relieving the stress and stimulating the healing processes.

Green Breathing

Lie down on your back and go through the relaxation response process. Once you have completely relaxed, imagine yourself lying in a cool, green forest glade. Everything around you is intensely green and beautiful. Now, as you breath through your nose, imagine that the greenness flows into your nostrils and down into your Tan Tien. As you breath in, notice how cooling the air feels. You can actually taste menthol in the green. Feel it circulate throughout your body, cooling and cleansing as it goes. As you breath in and out, imagine in your mind's eye that the green has become tinged with a dirty brown. These are the emotional toxins of stress leaving your body. Continue to breath in bright, clean green and to breath out nasty, dirty stress. Notice how revitalized you begin to feel, how utterly clean your body has become inside.

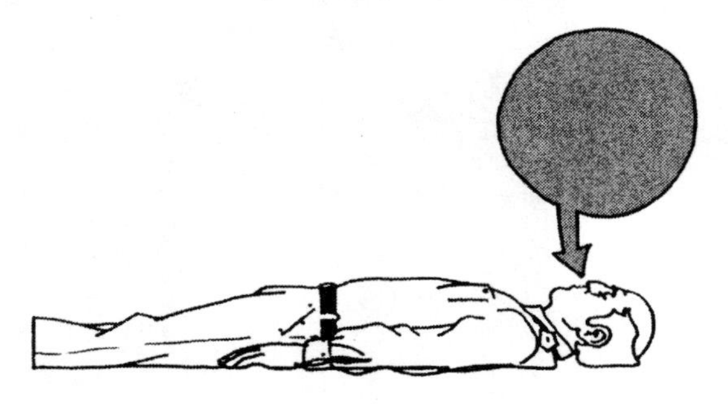

Breathing In Clean Green

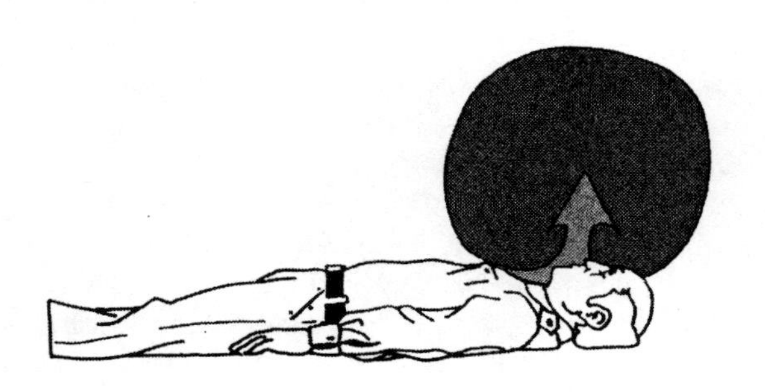

Breathing Out Dirty Green

Breathing Yellow

The next color breathing technique is done in exactly the same manner as the Green Breathing except this time lie on your back and visualize a bright yellow energy ball about the size of a basketball, floating over your head. Breath in the yellow. Allow it to descend to your Tan Tien and spread throughout your body. Notice how warm it makes you feel. As you breath out, picture the yellow becoming paler as its energy is tapped for use by your body. This is one way to energize your internal battery. This is an excellent exercise by which to relax and garner your strength before an escape attempt.

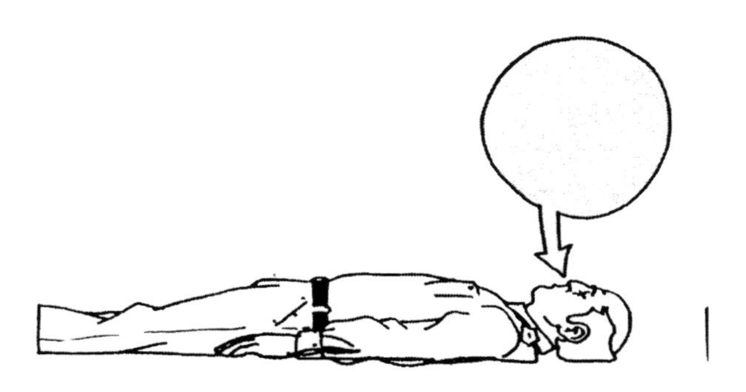

Breathing Yellow In

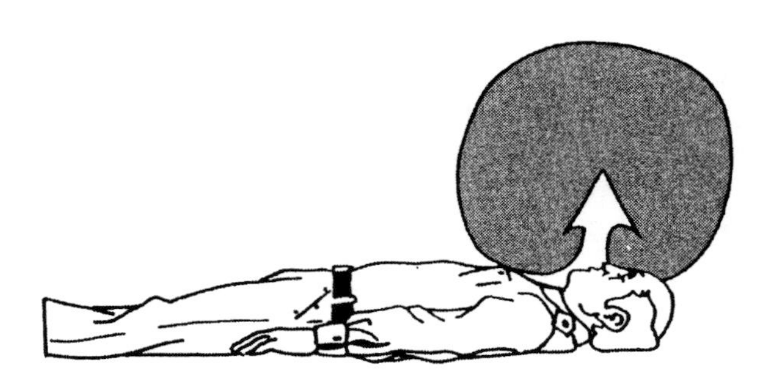

Breathing Out Dimmed Yellow

Orange Breathing

This last technique is designed to promote healing. Bob personally witnessed his teenaged son, Pat, cut the healing time of a broken ankle by about one third by using this technique. A sports psychologist and Aikidoist friend of Bob's from whom he learned this technique, used it to cut a broken leg's healing time in half. If you have sustained any injuries during your captivity, try using this color breathing technique, Don't worry about how or why it works, just know that it does!

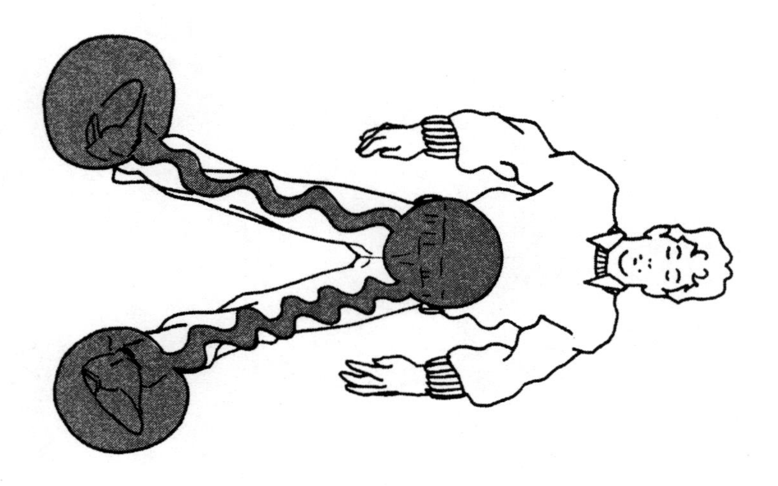

Orange Breathing

If the injury is in a leg, foot, or lower abdomen, imagine the yellow basketball of energy and use your mind to compress it to the size of a softball. As it shrinks, it will concentrate its energy and become bright orange. Imagine the orange energy ball floating in front of the sole of your left foot. As you breath in for six heart beats, picture your breath pulling the orange energy ball up through your left leg and into your Tan Tien area. Hold your breath for three heart beats, keeping the orange ball in your Tan Tien. Then, breath it out the right leg for six heart beats. On your next breath, breathe it up your right leg and out your left.

Continue breathing it back and forth while holding it in your Tan Tien between breaths.

If your injury is on an upper limb or chest, breath the orange energy ball through your hand and arm and down into the Tan Tien and then back out the other side. For a head, neck, or spine injury, engage the body circle that you used for breathing meditation.

As you breath the orange energy, think of its warmth acting both as a healing agent and an energizer. Do this several times a day for at least twenty minutes or longer. If you fall asleep, don't worry, the energy will continue to circulate and promote your healing as you sleep.

You now have several mental exercises that may prove useful for coping with captivity. You should practice them daily until you have thoroughly memorized the procedures and are feeling comfortable with their use. If you find useful applications for them in your daily life, please feel free to use them.

Language Study

If taken hostage, try to treat the experience in a positive manner. Use your idle time to increase your knowledge, health, and other capabilities. Richard Morefield, the overweight American Embassy hostage, said, [5] "...and if I'm smart, this (his exercise program) might have added ten years to my life."

One worthwhile activity might be to learn a language in your idle time. [6] Col Schaefer would study German from text books he had been given for 2 1/2 hours each morning. If you don't speak your captors' native language, take advantage of the Stockholm syndrome and ask them if they will teach it to you so that you can better understand their problems or causes. Of course, if knowing the local language helps you effect an escape later on, so much the better.

If there is a fellow hostage who can teach you a different language, learn it and use it as a means of secret communications between yourselves. You might find it handy while planning for your escape.

Playing With Your Captors' Minds

Depending on the intelligence level and sophistication of your captors' minds, it might be possible to play your captors against one another. It may also be possible to intimidate them. Two of the American Embassy Hostages in Iran, schoolmaster William Keough and Economist Robert Blucker both intimidated their captors. Keough treated his captors like recalcitrant pupils. [7] "Once we got over the initial pushing around, we established early on that this was not the thing to do... I spent quite a bit of time instructing people (his fellow hostages) on certain things they should know: How to push the limits, explaining to them that Iranian students understand confrontation, that we should be capturing the students rather than having them capture us." Blucker says of his guards by the end of the captivity, [8] "I had them so scared they were afraid to come into my room. I wouldn't let them in with their shoes on because they tracked in too much dirt. I yelled at them or I snarled at them. You could get to them by bitching at them."

Communications

[9] It is a common ploy for abductors to keep their captives separated from one another. This prevents them from discussing escape plans and wears down their morale. It is important for your mental welfare and for any hopes of escaping to be able to communicate with other prisoners. There are several ways this can be done; just like POWs and convicts have been doing for years.

Prison Mail

It is possible to establish communications with fellow captives by using common user areas, such as restrooms or exercise courtyards, for the passing of or leaving behind messages. A common place to leave a letter is inside the toilet paper roll's tube. You could put it inside a book as a quasi-bookmarker. The best places to use as mail drops are those places your captors expect you to use. You should change your hiding places frequently and also the times that you pick up and deliver your mail.

If you don't have writing materials, you can use charred wood, ashes mixed in just about any kind of fluid, or even some fruit juices for ink. Any kind of pointed object can be used as a pen. Toilet paper, cloth, leaves, cigarette papers, or wood can-be used for stationary.

Talking Walls

If someone is being held prisoner in a room next to yours, it's possible to carry on a quiet conversation through a wall common to both rooms. One way is to hold a drinking glass or cup with its bottom against the wall. Speak into the glass. The guy on the other side should hold the open end of his glass to the wall and place his ear onto the bottom of it. Another way is to roll a blanket up and bend it into the shape of a doughnut ring and place it against the wall. If you put you face into its center hole and speak slowly, it's possible for your voice to carry through to the other captive's glass receiver. This has the added benefit of being slightly more secure because the blanket will muffle your talking to the sides. It's also possible to talk out loud; however, it's much more dangerous. Sometimes it is possible to talk right in front of an abductor by using double-talk, street-jive, Rap, foreign languages not commonly spoken with your captors, or even a low level code such as Pig Latin (Ig-Pay AtinLay).

Tap Codes

Prisoners have used Tap Codes for years. Although the title refers to prisoners tapping on water pipes to transmit their messages, many other kinds of sounds could be used to include: whistling, blinking, coughing, and humming, tapping your foot, nudging the other guy, or even the rhythm of a broom's sweeping strokes.

Tapping is much easier than Morse code to learn and to operate. The system is based upon a matrix of letters- five cells across and five cells down. Yes, we know there are twenty-six letters in the alphabet. So that we can fit the whole alphabet into the twenty-five cell matrix, we double up and put "K" in with "C" (see the illustrations).

The way to use tapping is like this: Tap out the number of

Stacked Matrix

2. Then tap the column.

1. Tap the row.

	1	2	3	4	5
1	A	B	C/K	D	E
2	F	G	H	I	J
3	L	M	N	O	P
4	Q	R	S	T	U
5	V	W	X	Y	Z

the row containing the letter you want to use first, then tap out the number of that letter's column. For example, if you use a matrix containing the following rows of letters - First row =A B C/K D E, Second row = F G H I J, Third row=LMNOP, Fourth row=QRSTU, and Fifth row = V W X Y Z, and you want to spell out the word "GUARD", you would tap out 2/2 for G in the second row and the second column, 4/5 taps for U, 1/1 taps for A, 4/2 taps for R, and 1/4 taps for D. Make sure you give a short pause between the row and the column taps, a slightly longer pause between letters, a longer pause still between words.

If you want to be more sophisticated for security's sake, you can use a different arrangement of letters within the matrix. One very logical arrangement that may not be so readily apparent to a guard is the Rota System for arranging the alphabet. Instead of using nicely stacked rows of the alphabet's letters in left to right and top down order, try arranging them so that ABCDE is the top row, EFGHI is the right-hand column, NMLJI is the bottom row, AQPON is the left hand column, QRSTF is the second row, PYZUG is the third row, and OXWVH is the fourth row. The placement of letters is a spiral that goes around the outside and travels clock-wise in to the center cell of the matrix. The rota may start with A in any one of the four corners and spiraling clock-wise from that point. If you are able to work out a system like this with your fellow prisoners, you can use the first set of taps to indicate which cell "A" is in and then go from there.

ROTA MATRIX

	1	2	3	4	5
1	A	B	C/K	D	E
2	Q	R	S	T	F
3	P	Y	Z	U	G
4	O	X	W	V	H
5	N	M	L	J	I

Make sure you arrange for some administrative signals such as using a rapid series of taps to indicate that the message was not understood or not received, the receiver tapping twice to say he understands the word even if it hasn't been completed. This last helps cut down on transmission time.

The Spiritual Aspect

Being a hostage certainly isn't very much fun; however, if you make the most of the experience, you will gain from it. Both the Vietnam POWs and the Iranian hostages found great solace in spiritual meditations, study, and discussion. Kurt Krueger's experience was as much a spiritual one as it was an exercise in powerful meditating. If you happen to be religious, try regular prayer and study. Keep a small set of your favorite scriptures handy when you travel. Not only will the time pass easier, it will round out your self-improvement and leave you in a better emotional state. It will help you keep your hopes up. Remember, don't become a couch potato during captivity, keep physically, mentally, and spiritually fit so that you'll be ready to go when you are released or escape.

[1] McFadden, Treaster, & Carroll; *No Hiding Place,* 1981, The New York Times Company; P. 106-107.

[2] Ibid. P. 106

[3] Ibid. P. 107

[4] Ibid. P. 107

[5] Ibid. P. 107

[6] Ibid. P. 106

[7] Ibid. P. 103

[8] Ibid. P. 103

[9] "Special Forces Prisoner of War", *Combat Mission Magazine,* Nov 88, Vol. 1 Issue 4, P. 67.

CHAPTER 5

PLANNING THE ESCAPE

After overcoming or effectively handling the emotional and psychological effects of being taken hostage and learning to cope with captivity, an individual may start to consider the prospect of escaping. The decision whether to attempt an escape or not is personal and one which must be heavily weighed between the possibility of escaping and remaining free and the ramifications of the escape failing or in being recaptured after an initial escape. Such a decision could ultimately result in total freedom or death and should, therefore, not be made lightly.

Types of Escape

Four types of escapes/releases exist:

- Individual escape.
- Group escape.
- External force rescue.
- Abductor release.

While **individual escape** and **group escape** allow hostages the option of deciding whether to attempt an escape or not, **external force rescue** and **abductor release** provide no such option. Even so, in the latter two incidents, the hostage must be prepared to act rationally and quickly to insure personal survival. Such a requirement, as with the first two types of escape, demands mental and physical preparation and intensive planning to increase the possibility of successful escape and ultimate survival.

Individual Escape

When only one person is held hostage, the decision to escape is in fact a personal decision and offers the advantage of impacting on no other hostages. There is no need for the single hostage to concern himself with other hostages who might remain behind and yet still suffer the consequences for his escape or for those who might be recaptured in an attempted group escape. Additionally, it is much easier for one escaping hostage to hide or blend into his surroundings than it is for a group to do so. There are, however, negative aspects to an individual hostage escape attempt. An individual attempt means the captors can concentrate their guarding efforts on only one person. Additionally, one hostage attempting an escape eliminates the opportunity for joint planning and evaluating an escape plan. The old "two heads are better than one" approach isn't possible. Finally, an individual hostage escape provides a minimal sized force if it becomes necessary to overpower any guards.

Group Escape

Many of the negative aspects of an individual hostage escape attempt become positive in a group hostage escape attempt. A group of hostages requires the captors to concern themselves with the responsibilities of guarding more than one person. One good benefit is that planning doesn't necessarily have to be done in isolation. Over a period of time, escape plans can be discussed and assessed for the probability of success by all members of the group, thereby improving the validity of the plan selection process. If there comes a time when guards must be overpowered, a group will stand a better chance of successfully overwhelming them.

The major concern with a group escape is whether to attempt the escape if some of the hostages within the group will not or cannot go along. They would be left behind to face potential punishment and possible death in retribution for those who try and succeed. There is no simple answer to this dilemma, just as there is no simple answer to whether or not a single hostage should attempt an escape. This type of decision is situation dependent. Factors to be considered before making this decision are:

- Hostage treatment
- The possibility for eventual release
- The physical / mental condition of those to participate in the escape attempt.
- The condition of those that may have to stay behind.

If a hostage is being executed every hour, then an escape attempt is probably in order. After all, what would you have to lose? If most of the hostages involved in the escape attempt are in poor mental or physical condition, they shouldn't attempt an escape unless remaining behind would result in their sure death.

Rescue from Outside Forces

A rescue by an outside force such as a military Special Operations Force or a police SWAT team is another means for hostages to escape captivity. As stated earlier, an External Force Rescue is an escape leaving no choice to the hostage as to when or how. Yet you must be ready when an external force initiates its assault. Things may get rather exciting and dangerous. For instance, one type of scenario most sure to trigger external force action is if the abductors start systematically executing their hostages. If that happens, the authorities no longer have anything to lose in conducting an assault, so be prepared to react properly.

Your life could depend on the planning that you do for this contingency. While the primary purpose of an external force assault is to protect the life of the hostage and to gain his freedom, the assault usually results in a violent confrontation between the assaulting force and the captors.

Often an innocent hostage may be caught in the middle and frequently will become a casualty. Such was the case with the Dutch Marine raid in June, 1977, on a Dutch train in which 64 passengers were being held by South Moluccan terrorists. In the ensuing gun battle, one hostage was killed by the terrorists and another was shot by the Marines when he stood up in the train during the final assault.

Fifty-eight passengers lost their lives in an Egyptian Commando assault on an Egyptian airliner containing hostages held by terrorists on the island of Malta.

Abductor Release

While an abductor release requires no major physical effort on the part of the hostage to win his freedom, it is something he should be prepared for. Quite often abductors will release one or more hostages for any one or more of various reasons:

- To provide an initial means of communication with the legal authorities
- To gain public attention for a common cause
- To provide something in return for terms granted or promised by the negotiating authorities

An abductor release should never be refused unless accepting the release requires military personnel to do damage to their government!

There exist two potential psychological problems you may have to face as a released hostage. The first is a sense of guilt that you are now free while the others had to remain behind. This guilt can be greatly exacerbated if another hostage loses his or her life after your release. The second is finding yourself supporting the abductors because of the "Stockholm syndrome" causing a shift in your loyalties. These are significant and common to many hostage situations and should be talked through with a professional counselor as soon as possible.

Personal Assessment

Before a decision can be made about escaping, you must take stock of yourself. Do you have the mental/emotional and physical capabilities to execute an escape. Low morale and fear due to depression and stressful circumstances may deprive you of the confidence that you can successfully escape and remain free until you reach safety.

Concurrently, the lack of will or determination to do what must be done (including possibly having to kill a guard, steal a car, or to commit other acts not normally considered to be morally or legally proper) must be assessed.

In addition, the person planning an escape must determine whether or not he possesses the physical strength and skill to initiate an escape by overpowering or killing a guard and then running far enough to clear the area of captivity and avoid any ensuing search. You must also assess whether or not you possess the physical endurance allowing you to evade recapture until safety is reached. If you honestly feel that you or the other members of your escape party have the wherewithal in these areas of concern to successfully escape to freedom, it is now time to begin the substance of your escape plan.

Important Questions

Once a decision has been made to attempt an escape, a well thought out escape plan should be developed and mentally rehearsed until everyone concerned is thoroughly familiar with its execution and any contingency plans in case of its disruption. The escape plan should be rationally thought out and structured in minute detail. There are several important questions for which the answers will form the foundation of the escape plan structure:

- How to escape?
- When to escape?
- How to stay free?
- Where to go once initially free?
- How to get there?

These are all questions one must attempt to answer in an escape plan. In many cases, a hostage will not know where he is since he may have been blindfolded during his travel to the confinement site. In criminal situations other than kidnappings, such as a bank holdup hostage situation, the hostage will probably know exactly where he is being held so this is not as big a challenge as it might be in a terrorist or a kidnapping abduction. Concurrently with the possibility of not knowing where one is held, you may not know where to go nor whom to trust once you have made your initial escape. This is especially true in such places as Beruit, Lebanon, where there are many factions that look alike, share the same or similar neighborhoods, and work on agendas entirely of their own choosing (which may or may not match a hostage's).

Information Gathering

In the military, we learn to develop plans based upon two major ingredients: the mission (which in your case is to get away and stay that way) and intelligence which includes not only the enemy's capabilities and intentions but the battleground itself.

You should begin your escape planning by trying to determine to some degree of certainty where you are and what time of day it is. This might not mean you'll know the street address where you're being held captive; however, by listening for sounds such as traffic noises and factory noises, you can ascertain whether you are being held in a built-up area, a rural setting, near an airport or a train track, etc. This determination can help greatly in the development of the escape plan.

If you determine that you are being held in a congested city area, once initially free, you might be able to quickly lose yourself in the congestion of people, buildings, markets, and traffic of the urban community. A city also allows you a better chance of finding help in terms of the police or military.

On the other hand, if you determine that you are being held in a rural area, realize that the escape plan must include the possibility of having to travel and sleep in the woods or hills for days without a sure supply of food and potable water until you can find help.

Determining the type of captivity area and approximate times of the day will provide you the first bits of information needed to plan an escape. If held in the city, you could plan your escape to coincide with rush hour congestion which may allow you to quickly lose yourself in its confusion. An escape at night time (when the guards are probably more sleepy and vulnerable to being overwhelmed) provides darkness of night, buildings, and dark alleys as concealment to aid your flight from captivity.

By the Numbers

You must then plan the specific execution steps of the escape. This is by far the most critical portion of the plan. If it fails, it offers the greatest possibility for personal injury or death to the escapee. If constantly guarded, you must assess when and which guards offer the greatest opportunities for trickery or overpowering. Realistically, the best guard shift for our purposes is when only one or the weakest guard or the most trusting guard is on duty. This offers an advantage to the hostage.

You should also carefully review what weapons are maintained by the guards and where they are located. Do you know how to use the guard's weapon? If not, it will be of little use to you and could prove harmful later on. If you took a weapon and didn't know how to use it or had no intention to use it, your pursuers might consider you armed and dangerous. They might shoot first and ask questions later.

Finally, in respect to guards, you must determine what level of force you are willing to use to overcome them:

- Should you attempt to overpower and physically re strain the guard?
- Should you knock him out?
- Should you kill him?

This decision is crucial from two points of view. Merely restraining or knocking out the guard offers the guard the possibility of quick recovery and the chance to alert others and/or to pursue the escapee. Killing the guard, however, eliminates these possibilities but increases the likelihood of personal harm or death if you are recaptured.

Other considerations in determining how to execute the escape include:

- Determining a primary route and where possible,
- A secondary route of exit from the captivity site. The best way to determine the beginnings of these routes is to attempt to move around your area of confinement while you make a surreptitious reconnaissance. Logical cover reasons for moving around could be exercise or to go to the toilet.

Look for routes that would allow for rapid, silent, concealed movement away. American journalist Charles Glass was given some rather anxious moments when he made his initial escape from a Beirut apartment without the advance knowledge of what lay beyond his room. Once he freed himself from some ankle chains, the only way out of his room other than through its one interior door was a shuttered balcony door that had a wooden wardrobe blocking it. Glass said:

[1] "I inched the wardrobe away from the shutter door, stopping when the wood squeaked. At last I could open the door, and squeeze out onto the balcony. I gazed upon the world outside my cell. The sky was clear, the night was warm and still, and the streets seemed deserted. I took a deep breath of air and looked down: it was a straight drop of six or seven stories.

The only way off the balcony, other than back to my room, was through a door that led to the kitchen. I stepped inside, walked quietly through the kitchen and into the main corridor, where I could see the open door of the guards' bedroom.

Turning left, I headed toward the front door. Slowly I turned the key to unlock it. There were two bolts, which I pulled back. I turned the handle and moved the door slowly toward me. Then I slipped out, taking the key and locking the door behind me. I ran down the stairs, out the building's entrance, and up the asphalt road."

The route should also provide some form of cover or protection in case shooting starts. Such cover will be valuable in that it would offer an escaping hostage a place from which to return fire if he has acquired a weapon or a safe position from which to surrender if the plan goes awry. It should, if possible, include an exit passage usually unlocked such as a door or a window. And finally, the route should support the follow-on portion of the plan. For example, if the follow-on portion of the plan is to quickly blend into a congested street of people and vehicles, going out a back door into an alley may not offer the speed of blending in that exiting a front door might allow.

Blending In

A further consideration in escape planning is the ability to

Growing hair to blend in better.

blend in with your surroundings once you get free. This may not be a major consideration when escaping from a spur of the moment criminal situation; however, it is extremely important if you are an American being held hostage in the Middle East. An extended period of captivity will allow your hair and beard to grow. Such growth allows an American to blend in much better with Middle Eastern natives than does a clean-shaven, short-haired look. This is true in other parts of the world as well.

Clothing is very important when attempting to blend in. If it is similar to the native dress of the area in which you are being held, you will greatly increase your chances for blending in and remaining free. You should attempt to acquire native clothing over a period of time by casually requesting a native piece of apparel now and then from your captors. After all, you'll need a change of clothing if your captivity lasts for any significant period of time.

After your escape, you could steal a change of clothing from off someone's wash line as soon as any opportunity presented itself.

Longer Range Planning

Once you've determined the best time of day for an escape attempt based upon guard vulnerability and outside activity; once you have determined the method and level of force you will have to use to overpower the guard; once you have decided whether to take and use any available weapon; once you have selected primary and secondary routes of escape; and once you have planned for blending into your surroundings, you have completed planning for your initial escape. Now you must plan for your continued escape and flight to safety.

If held hostage in a criminal situation such as a bank holdup or prison revolt, you will probably have a fair knowledge of the area outside of the confinement area. Additionally, once free, you will probably only have to continue your escape to awaiting law enforcement officials who will have the immediate area cordoned off to prevent the captors' escape. Such knowledge and availability of law enforcement officials limits the requirement to plan for continued escape in detail. The most important planning aspect in this type of situation is selecting a continued escape route, which provides some cover and concealment from your captors' line of fire. Having knowledge of the area would really help here.

For those held hostage in a kidnap or a terrorist situation, things are different. They are usually held in captivity with no knowledge of the area outside the place of confinement other than a guess as to whether it is in a city or a rural area. If you are in this type of situation, you will have very little factual knowledge to support continued-escape planning. Your plan for a continued escape will probably be brief and general in concept until you actually initiate the escape and have time to assess your whereabouts.

Planning for your continued escape must include actions to keep you free. You must determine what or who will be the objective guaranteeing your ultimate freedom and safety. Using what the US Army calls "Reverse Sequence Planning", a method by which the Army first identifies an objective and then plans in reverse from that objective back to the initial start point to insure each phase of planning will lead to and support the next phase. You should determine what or who it is that can provide freedom and safety, and based upon that determination, plan those things which will keep you free long enough to reach this objective. For instance, if you decide that the first policeman you see is that objective, then your plan for continued escape should allow you to quickly blend in with your surroundings and to continue to move until you locate a policeman to whom you can turn yourself in.

If, on the other hand, you don't trust the local police and feel that you must find an embassy, consulate, or an agency friendly to your nationality, then your plan will necessarily be longer in range. It must call for quickly blending in with your surroundings; possibly finding a hiding place for rest and food. This is especially important in a rural area where you may have to travel for days to reach a city.

The plan for continued escape should also consider a mode of travel. If required (particularly in a rural setting), stealing an available vehicle will offer speed of travel. It may also bring official attention upon you from the police so there are several tradeoffs to consider here.

In a large city, your plan for travel may initially include foot movement to quickly clear the area of captivity followed by flagging a taxi and asking to be taken to the nearest friendly embassy or consulate since taxi drivers usually know their cities and drive quickly.

Bob knows a young female Army Sergeant who was kidnapped for a while on a train from Stuttgart to Munich, Germany by Turkish gangsters and white slavers. They had walked into her compartment and held her against her will. When they stopped in the Munich train station, they started guiding her off the train. Having acted scared and complacent up to that point, she caused them to drop their guard long enough for her to jerk away and run screaming to the nearby taxi stand. A driver quickly threw her and her things into the cab and took off for the nearest police station.

There, she was able to give accurate descriptions of both the men. Within 24 hours, the efficient Munich Kriminal Polizei (criminal police) managed to apprehend the two who had long records for various gangster activities. They are presently serving some long, hard time behind bars. Had it not been for an alert taxi driver, she might have been a captive prostitute in some Middle Eastern bordello.

A hostage planning a getaway must have a plan for continuing his escape which will take him out of the area of captivity This takes him out of the abductors' immediate search area and provides him with an objective to strive for that maintains his present freedom and eventually provides his ultimate freedom and safety.

Planning for the Abductor Release

The most important thing you can do in anticipation of this eventuality is to constantly observe your captors and their activities and habit patterns. Memorize everything you can about them so that you can pass on as much usable information to the negotiating authorities as possible. This also includes information about the containment area, which could prove critical to an assault team's plans. Remember, you may be the only source of inside, up to date knowledge about what the authorities are facing. Try to help them help others.

Planning For an External Force Rescue

As stated earlier, the hostage has no direct control over a rescue by an external force. Additionally, in most cases of external force rescues, you will have no prior notice of the impending rescue attempt. Quite often hostages become the innocent victims of their rescuers when the rescue force confronts the captors and a shoot-out occurs. You can; however, plan certain passive and active measures, which may save your life during a rescue confrontation.

Passive Measures

Passive planning should first include the assumption that your abductors won't release you and you cannot escape. A second assumption should be that once your location is known, a rescue attempt will be made. Based on these initial assumptions, certain passive measures should be planned and practiced. The first of these is to make it a point to always sit or lie down when in your captors' presence, unless they don't allow you to do so. You should also try to keep as far away from them as possible.

These actions alone could save your life during a rescue attempt by keeping you out of the line of fire between the captors and the rescue force.

Another passive measure that you should attempt is to maintain a cordial and respectful relationship with your captors. The establishment of a human bond between hostage and captor may deter the captor from executing the hostage when he realizes a rescue is taking place. It is much harder to murder someone with whom a friendly bond has been developed than it is to murder someone who argues and is defiant. Several Jewish hostages during the Entebbe Raid owe their lives to a German terrorist with whom they had earlier made to feel ashamed for his countrymen's actions during the holocaust. When the Israeli Commandos stormed the airport buildings, he looked at them as if ready to execute them. One of the hostages asked him if he was like the Nazis. That reminder was enough for him to turn from them and defiantly go down in a blazing gun battle with the Commandos rather than to harm his charges.

A final passive measure is to always be alert for signals that a rescue attempt is about to take place.

Active Measures

Planning active measures to take during a rescue attempt is extremely important. The first action a hostage should take upon realizing that a rescue attempt has commenced is to immediately lie face down and attempt to remain motionless and silent. You should not try to physically or verbally make contact with the rescue force. Any such attempt could result in your being mistaken for a resisting captor and getting shot. You may also draw vindictive attention from your captors. You should allow yourself to be apprehended by the rescue force and taken from the place of captivity. There will be time later to identify yourself as a former hostage and have that identity verified.

The passive and active measures identified above are simple to plan and easy to implement; however, hostages have been injured or killed more frequently than necessary simply because they failed to plan for and implement these measures for their own safety. Such a small effort for such a big price to pay!

Conclusion

Escaping from captivity is a personal decision. You must weigh the possibility of escaping against your escape failing thus resulting in tragedy. Just as important is your evaluation of your chances for survival and ultimate release. Mental/emotional and physical capabilities to execute the escape must be assessed. If you determine that you are capable of executing an escape and that your chances for survival and freedom are good, you must plan logically and in detail for all contingencies. Given proper planning, a thorough assessment of both yourself and your captors, and a strong desire to survive an escape to freedom, you will have the best possible chance for freedom should an opportunity for escape, release, or rescue arise.

[1] Charles Glass, "Kidnapped In Beirut", *The Readers' Digest*, April 1988, (Condensed from *Rolling Stone*), P.96.

CHAPTER 6

PHYSICAL RESISTANCE

Knowing Your Limitations

There may come a time during your captivity when you might consider using violence to effect your escape. If you are not well trained, if the timing is wrong, if you are not committed to following through on your actions, you may get injured or killed, or you may cause others to be hurt or killed.

You must know your limitations! If you are older and/or not in good shape, you need to understand that your reflexes will not be as fast or as smooth as you remembered them when you took that karate course 20 years ago. Pride lets us see ourselves in the best possible light. That could be lethal!

The hostage takers may be younger than you; he or she may have had a recent intensive course in hand-to-hand combat; and they are more emotionally hyped thereby increasing their speed with adrenaline. If they have initiated the taking of hostages, they may have planned out every aspect of it and are expecting trouble while you have no forewarning and can only react. They may be more desperate, considering they have nothing to lose as is the case of a "Lifer" convict or a criminal who has just killed someone.

You must consider these and many other aspects before you attempt physical violence! If there is the slightest chance of hesitation or fumbling on your part, you may be better off not trying anything! If the captors are Middle Eastern, go for it.

Consideration of Fellow Hostages

If you deem it necessary to use physical violence (for instance, the captors have already killed or wounded others for seemingly no reason and they seem about ready to do it again), first consider the possible impacts your actions may have on any other fellow hostages. Will they be inadvertently harmed by your actions or through the captors' retaliation after your attempt, whether it is successful or not?

If there is a gun involved, might it discharge in the direction of innocent people? If there is a grenade or bomb involved, is it worth wrestling with the captor? Is there a safe place to throw it should you gain control of it? How long a delay will there be once the firing mechanism has been triggered?

There's more involved than one might think when weighing the chances of successfully overpowering a captor or a guard. For instance, when Bob trains security guards and Military Police in foiling assassination attempts, he uses disarming techniques that turn weapons such as guns back into the wielder so that only the attacker is endangered in the fray. If you feel physical resistance techniques are called for, please consider the safety of innocent bystanders.

When and If To Use Violence

Escaping a hostage situation is similar to escape in a prisoner of war situation. One must do it immediately during the capture process while a high state of confusion exists. Or, you should wait until later after there is time for careful planning and when the guards are possibly less vigilant. It is common for terrorists to kill or injure someone soon after the incident begins to prove they mean business. If a chance to use physical resistance comes early on, you might first want to reconsider your capabilities in comparison with those manifested by the hostage takers. If you don't, instead of saving the guy they were going to make an example of, they'll make you the example. In the case of a criminal, you might want to hold back because they don't generally kill right away since they need hostages for self-protection. The terrorist, on the other hand, is more interested in making a media splash and will do just about anything to get it.

If the captor is systematically killing off people or if he appears insane and begins dehumanizing his victims by covering their faces with masks or hoods, you may be forced into physical resistance action simply out of self-preservation. As a general rule, however, a victim should remain passive and avoid eye contact with the assailants thus living to fight another day. No one admires dead heroes or bumblers who cause injury or death to them selves or other victims. Examine your motives before acting rashly.

You must also be careful in that there may be more opponents than you realize. Sometimes terrorists use a "sleeper" agent (a fellow terrorist) who watches the victims' initial reactions for signs of "trouble makers" before he shows his true colors. Be aware of this possible danger!

The safest time for physical resistance is when guards have been lulled into carelessness. On two different occasions, an American OSS agent was able to escape from his Gestapo captors by using a pencil to kill the lone Nazi interrogator left with him to obtain a confession. Since the prisoner had looked so helpless, no one assumed that he would attempt to overcome a lone, armed guard. How ironic that the guard actually handed the prisoner the very implement by which he lost his own life.

Timing is Everything

One of the most important elements of physical resistance is timing. There are two aspects to this:

- One is the timing of the attempt itself.
- The other is during the execution of the physical resistance technique used.

The first has already been discussed previously on when and if to use violence. The second is related to the tempo of the technique's execution. If you initially move slowly and clumsily when you're around the captors, you will have an advantage if you have to explode suddenly into action later. Bob, who is a slow moving bear of a guy, usually surprises sparring partners when he suddenly ups the tempo of a practice session and allows his true speed to come forth. The same can happen in a real fight where an assailant becomes overconfident due to misjudging an opponent's capabilities. By executing your resistance techniques when the captor is least expecting them and by moving faster than expected, your chances for success will be greatly enhanced.

Commitment

If you decide that you must use violence, do not hesitate, go for broke! The worst thing that you can do in hand-to-hand combat is to begin an attack, thereby alerting your opponent to danger, and then hesitating, allowing the opponent to regain the initiative. Using violence to escape a hostage situation is very similar to a woman using violence to escape a rape situation. Once the violence has been initiated, the level of violence throughout the whole situation rises.

If your attack is not successful, expect a very violent (possibly fatal) retaliation. If you are not committed to maiming or killing another human being, DO NOT START ANYTHING! If you cannot come to grips with blinding (with your thumbs if need be) your captor, or crushing his larynx so he chokes to death, or dislocating his knee, or breaking his arm, don't attack him. There are no such things as "fair" or "foul" targets or techniques as found in "Sport Karate". Anything goes and you must be committed to getting there first with the most in order to survive and win. This is a contest of win or die.

In many of Bob's women-only rape escape clinics, some students shudder when he graphically describes how to drive one's thumbs into the inside corners of an attacker's eyes and to scoop out his eyeballs. Bob says, "If you cannot deal with the emotions and ethics required to execute deadly techniques, do not resist your attacker in any way. To do so and fail will earn you a ferocious beating at best and quite possibly death."

In one rape escape clinic, Bob asked whether anyone had been attacked and whether they cared to share their experience with the class. A sweet-faced 83 year old lady held up her hand and told this chilling story:

She had recently moved into a one-story four-plex apartment complex for the elderly. One night, about three A.M., she awoke and noticed that her outdoors security light was no longer reflecting off her hallway wall outside her bedroom door. As she lay quietly in bed, wondering how the light was turned off, a man's figure suddenly silhouetted itself in the doorway for what seemed like ten hours but was only ten minutes. He suddenly turned and walked away down the hallway.

The lady was too petrified to move from her bed until sunrise when she finally worked up enough courage to check out the apartment. He was gone and the outside door was locked. Because there was no evidence of a break-in, she did not report the incident.

The next night she made sure her door was locked and the security light was on and then went to bed. Again she awoke to find this time the man was sitting on her bed, staring down at her. Again she played possum, pretending to be asleep, with the exception of her hand which she stealthily eased up under her pillow.

What the intruder didn't know was that he had selected a gutsy old lady of hardy pioneer stock. While he was staring down at her, she had closed her hand around the handle of a flat-bladed screwdriver that she had placed under her pillow before going to sleep.

Fortunately for him, he didn't make any aggressive moves; he simple stared at her for twenty minutes and then arose and left. Had he made a wrong move, she had been determined to plunge the screwdriver into his throat. Surprise and darkness would never have allowed him to see it coming. She was totally committed to defending herself.

After the police installed a deadbolt lock the next day, they determined that the intruder was either a worker or a friend or relative of a worker around the complex who had gained access to a master key. In any case, he never got in again.

Follow Through

One of the first concepts taught in most sports and in the martial arts is the idea of follow through. There are two manifestations:

First is the aspect of a technique's execution. A baseball batter knows he must allow the swing of his bat to follow through the natural arc of a circle even after hitting the ball. The same applies to a golfer. In the martial arts, we learn to think beyond or through the target in a like manner. If you are striking at a vulnerable target such as a throat, you must pretend that the target is 6-12 inches behind its actual location. The reason for this is psychological in nature. As your hand nears the actual target, your subconscious mind thinks, "You might hurt your hand so you better start slowing up." If you think through your target, you'll still be accelerating as your hand hits, insuring a maximally delivered force. One that is deadly!

Thinking Through the Target

The second aspect of follow through concerns multiple techniques. Generally speaking, the initial attack will not be enough. You must strike boldly with surprise and keep on attacking until the captor is down and cannot get back up. In Bob's martial art, Korean Hapkido, there exists a set of fighting strategies or principles called Water Theory. One aspect of this is the nature of water to enlarge even small holes in a barrier such as a dam or a submarine hull. Just as water may enlarge a small opening into a gaping tear, your initial attack will create other openings into vulnerable targets, which will lead to even more openings as you attack each new opportunity. For example, if you knee a man in the groin, he will bend over slightly and grab his genitalia in reflex. This action brings his hands and arms down leaving his facial area open. Striking his unprotected ear holes simultaneously with your cupped hands will disorient him even further, allowing you plenty of time to dislocate his knee with a kick, and so on. Never stop with just one technique!

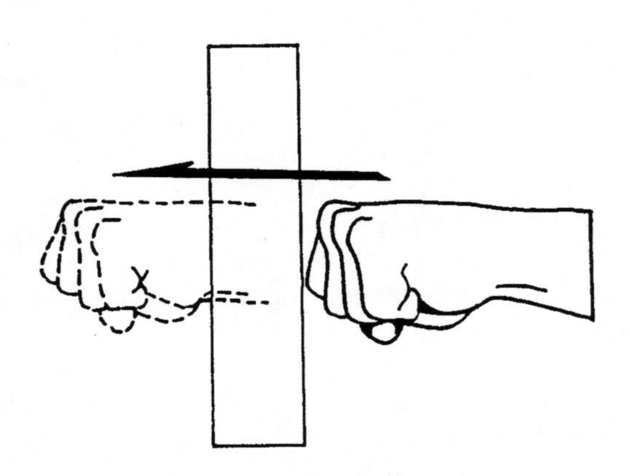

Thinking Through the Target

Vulnerable Target Areas

The interesting aspect of hand-to-hand fighting is that one needn't be a super athlete to be effective. If you have prepared for the physical resistance properly by pretending to be weak, slow, pacific, and/or handicapped, and if you have waited for the right opportunity, you will have surprise on your side. If you couple this surprise factor to a series of attacks to the captor's weakest, most vulnerable points, you stand a good chance of immobilizing him.

There are actually over a hundred vulnerable points on the body. Obviously you would have to train for many hours to master pinpoint precision for attacking all of them. Since this book is directed toward those men or women who may never have had

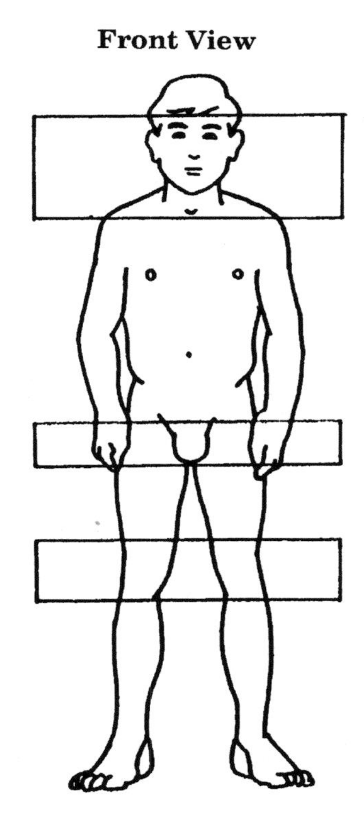

Eyes

Throat (Adam's apple)

Groin

Knees

an opportunity to study a martial art at length, we have selected only a few of what the military would term as "high value" or "high payoff" targets that can be easily learned and remembered. The illustrations on the next page portray these points. For those who may desire a more comprehensive knowledge base, we recommend Bob's video instruction tapes and books. For an in-depth, comprehensive and highly technical reference, we recommend Bob's book, [1] *Hapkido: The Integrated Fighting Art.*

Your Dangerous Body

As was the case for vulnerable target areas, we did not wish to inundate the reader with too many ways in which one can use the body to kill or maim. For this reason the illustrations following the vulnerable points provide a bare bones approach to personal combat attacks. We purposely did not include any de-

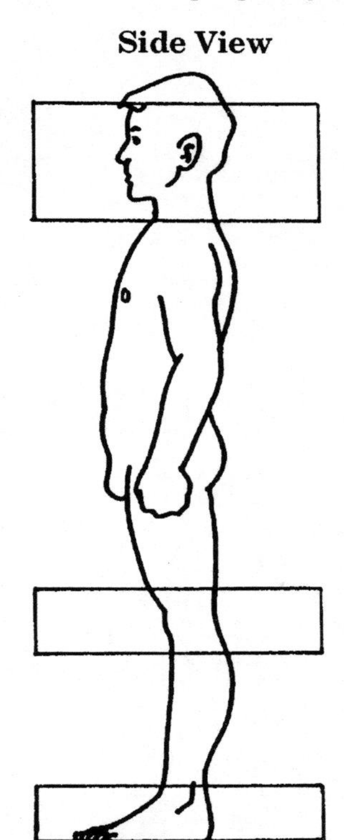

Ear holes

Side of neck

Side of knee

Ankles and feet

Physical Resistance

Back view

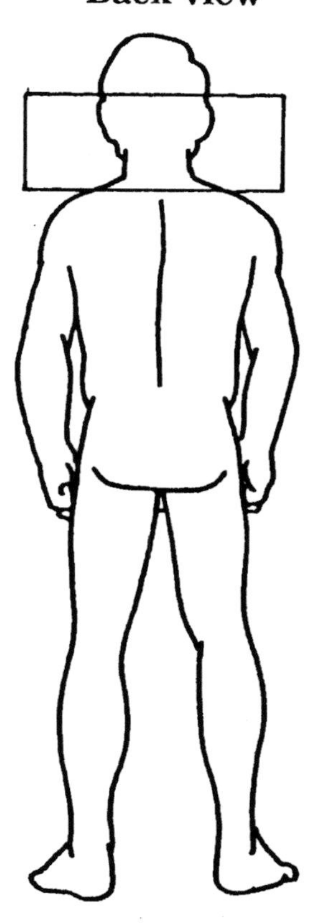

Base of skull

Neck

fenses since that is too complex for the purposes of escaping a hostage situation. The idea is to surprise the captor with a devastating attack and to relentlessly pursue follow-up techniques before he can recover. If the initial attack is not successful, you are probably outclassed and will soon be "dead meat" regardless of any defenses you might try. Again, for more details of possibilities, we recommend Bob's resources (see the resource section at the end of this book).

The following are some of the martial arts' most devastating attacks that can be performed adequately by novices of either sex. We have attempted to provide at least one per each vulnerable target area.

Eye Gouge Out

1. Plunge your thumbs into the inside corners of his eyes as deep as they will go.

2. Scoop your thumbs to the outside popping his eyeballs out of his head.

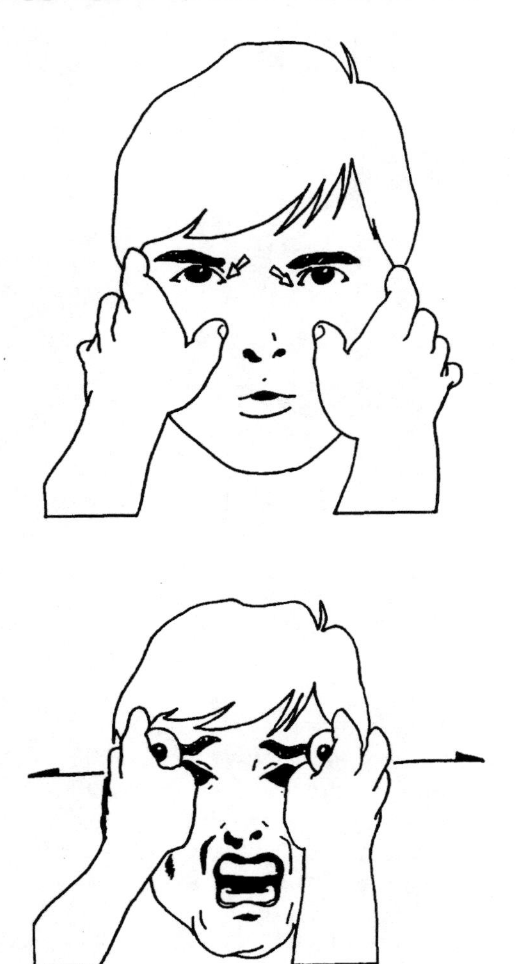

Knife Edge of Hand to Throat

1. Cock your stiffened hand across your body.

2. Lash out the knife edge of the hand against his Adam's apple.

Palm Strike Neck Break

1. **Grab him by the lapels with one hand pulling him in toward you.**

2. **Strike him on the chin straight forward and slightly upwards with the palm of your hand while pulling him forward until his neck breaks.**

Cupped Hands to Ear Holes

1. Cup your hands and.....

2. slam them simultaneously over both ear holes creating an overpressure which breaks the ear drums and causes extreme pain and disorientation.

Knee to Groin

1. Grab your enemy and.....

2. bring your knee up as hard as you can into his groin while pulling him forward.

Low Side Kick to Knee

1. Cock your leg across your body and.....

2. strongly snap-thrust the outside of your foot down and out against the side, front, or back of his knee to dislocate/break it.

Rear Neck-Breaker Take Down

1. This is a silent sentry-neutralization technique. Sneaking up from behind, cover his mouth and pinch his nostrils shut.

2. Pull him back toward you while you punch him powerfully in the kidney.

3. Slip your hand down bringing your arm across his throat while pulling him back.

4. Clasp your own hand tightly into a choke, throw your feet back while maintaining the choke so that you both land on the ground breaking his neck.

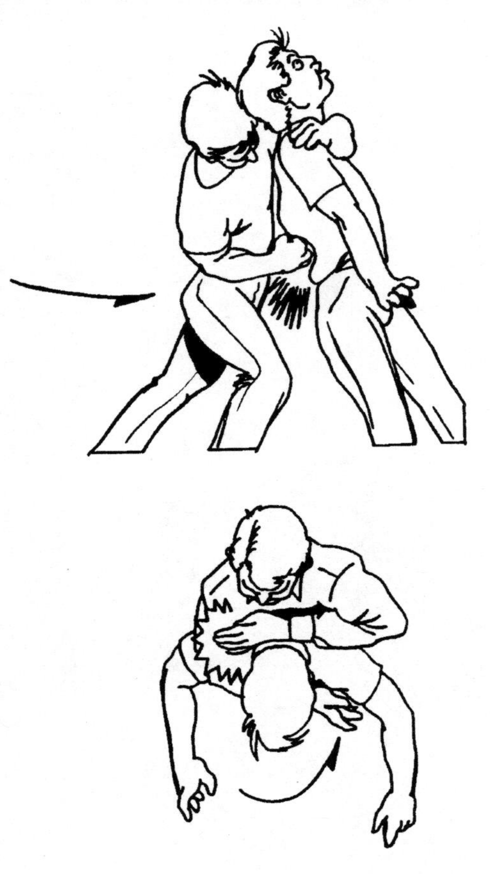

Front Bar-Arm Choke

1. Place one of your forearms against his neck, grabbing your own upper arm and.....

2. wrap your other arm around the back of his neck and squeeze your arms together in a vice to choke the life out of him.

Physical Resistance

The Importance of Aggressiveness

The concepts of being committed, follow through, and the knowledge of how to fight dangerously are directly related to being aggressive or inculcating the warrior spirit. An Israeli sports psychologist told an incredible story to Bob about two ten-year-old Israeli boys on a kibutz who were caught out in the open by two Arab terrorists. The boys were unarmed and the terrorists, both men in their early twenties, each had a knife. The boys did not give up in abject fear but fought for their lives like young lion cubs, using fighting knowledge they had been given in their training on the kibutz. The boys got cut, severely so, but they managed to demoralize and route the two terrorists who actually ran away when they realized that these boys were bravely carrying the fight to them. The kids fought aggressively despite being totally overmatched and managed to survive with their lives, while the terrorists showed their cowardly nature. If they hadn't demonstrated that they were willing to fight to the death, they would have been cruelly murdered.

Expedient Weapons

The ancient samurai warriors never fought with their bare hands if a weapon was at hand despite the fact they were masters of unarmed combat. The same should hold true for an escaping hostage. Many everyday items can be turned into deadly weapons when applied properly. In 1987, Bob's sixteen-year-old daughter (5'1", 110 lbs) saved a college girl from being raped by judiciously breaking a heavy glass beer stein over the attacker's shoulder. She hit him so hard, he passed out from shock on the sidewalk. The following pictures illustrate how to turn common household items into deadly weapons that may give you an edge when you really need it.

Throw boiling water or soup into his face (soup is better because it tends to stick to his skin more than water does.

If you are being carjacked, don't forget you are driving a wonderful expedient weapon. If you were foolish enough to leave your doors or windows open and a carjacker starts to get in, put the car into reverse and floor it. Then thrust it into drive and floor it again. You may damage the read end of your car, but you will also damage the heck out of the carjacker. You get bonus points if you run over his legs.

If he does get in, assuming you have your seatbelt on and

Backhand a large mug into his face or hammer it down onto his head or collar bone.

Use a chair to strike him at the base of the skull.

Throw boiling water or soup into his face (soup is better because it tends to stick to his skin more than water does.

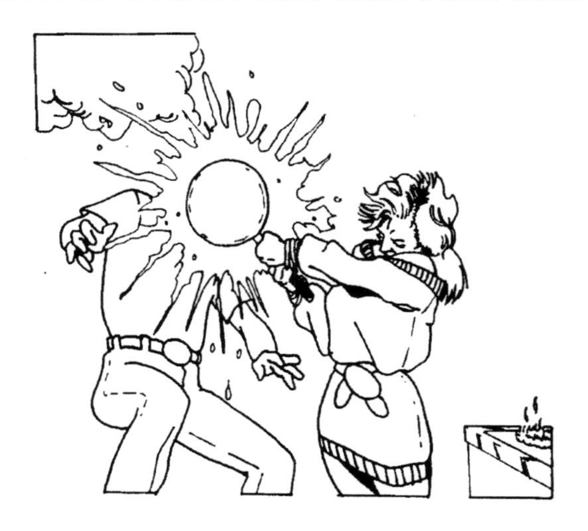

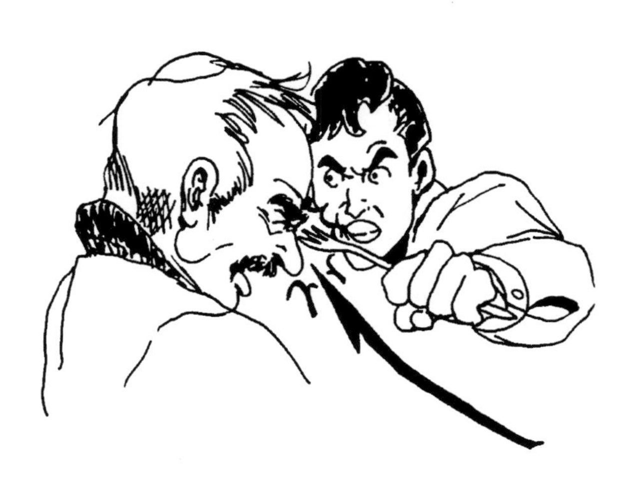

Thrust a table fork into his eye!

1. Place a pencil between the first two fingers and abut the eraser-end into the base of your thumb.

2. Close your fist.

3. Thrust the sharpened end into his jugular in the front-side of his neck, or in his eye, or under his Adam's apple in his throat.

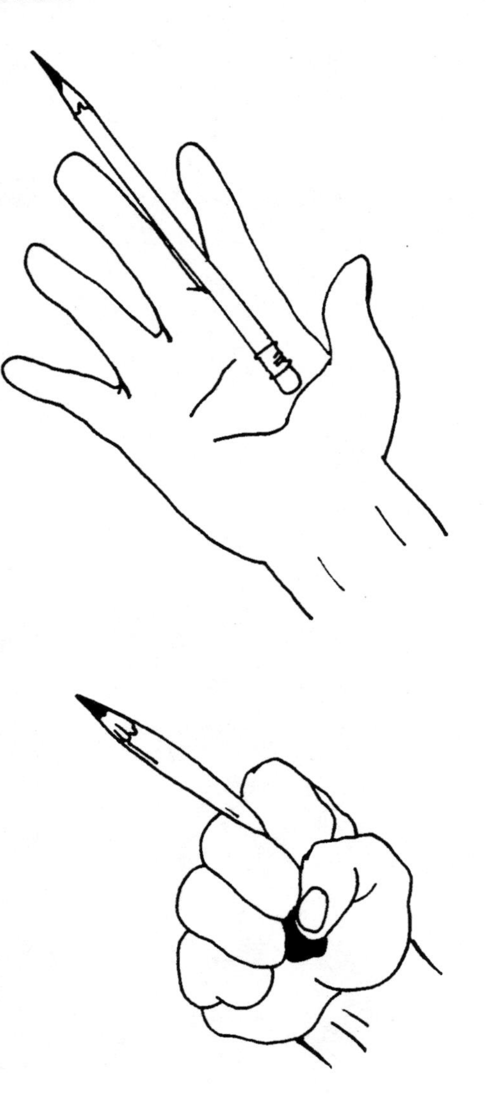

Hold an open flame about three inches in front of the nozzle of an aerosol spray can. Spray across the flame and crisp his face with your improvised flame thrower.

Roll up a magazine tightly and use it as a thrusting weapon into your enemy's throat.

he doesn't, run into a pole or a building at about 20-25 mph. Get out and run away. It's doubtful he will be able to follow.

If the Captor Has a Weapon

There exist many excellent techniques for dealing with knives, pistols, rifles, or clubs; however, these all require intense training under the guidance of a qualified instructor. This is a case of a little knowledge being too dangerous to the user. If the captor has a weapon, you should not take him on unless he's asleep or otherwise incapacitated. If he has a hand grenade or a bomb, don't fight him under any circumstances since many innocent bystanders could be killed or wounded. Again, if you have a deep interest in techniques against weapons, we refer you to Bob's martial art books and video tapes which deal extensively with this area of concern.

Martial Art Usefulness

Does the studying of a martial art automatically make one a killer, able to defend himself in any situation? Certainly not! Too many people naturally assume that satisfying the requirements for a black belt makes them an expert. It doesn't! In fact, reaching first-degree black belt merely means one has mastered the basics of his art. There are usually seven to nine more levels of black belt to go before the Grand Master level is attained. Each degree may represent as much or more time in study and teaching as the first degree did. For example, the US Hapkido Federation requires six years time in grade between 5th and 6th degree black belt levels.

Many an overconfident black belt has found himself on the losing end of a battle with an experienced street fighter. Too often, attaining a black belt means having memorized twenty sets of sequential dance-like movements called forms or katas plus having demonstrated a moderate ability to freespar according to sport karate rules. A program such as this does not train a student for street or battlefield survival. Now please don't misinterpret these statements. There are certainly many benefits to be gained from the above program, such as:

- weight control and enhanced health
- an ability to concentrate
- self confidence

We feel, however, programs such as these can lead to a false sense of security. We are not addressing a student's need to feel good about themselves, but his/her need for programming them into an effective fighting machine that can render another human being powerless in as short a time as possible.

Not all arts can do this. Soft arts such as Aikido and Tai Chi are either too passive, seeking only to control violence, or are basically an exercise system. Many of the hard arts, on the other end of the spectrum, have become too "sportized" or too hung up on ineffective classical movements that may not pertain to the needs of the street. Too many arts advocate spending long hours of practice on ancient farmer implement weapons that are either illegal or too impractical to carry around on one's person.

Does this mean that it is fruitless to study a martial art? Absolutely not! One should; however, choose a style that concentrates on street survival. Such styles include integrated arts as Korean Hapkido, Hwarangdo, and Kooksulwon; Japanese Jiujitsu and Ninjitsu; and Chinese Wing Chun and Chin Na.

In fact, it doesn't have to be a formal or classical style. Many schools now teach combinations of several styles. Some train only for the street. If a school displays numerous trophies and brags about tournament participation, it may be too sports oriented. There is one school in the Monterey, California area that is called the "Mug-A-Model Course". This school is famous for teaching women how to become vicious fighters as a rape prevention measure. The course lasts about six weeks and allows women to hit and kick at full strength and speed at heavily padded male attacker role players. One of the best testimonials for this training approach is the story of one school graduate who found herself attacked by a rapist eight years after she had attended the "Mug-A-Model Course". Although she had had zero reinforcement and no additional training in the intervening eight years, she was able to react instinctively. Within the first five seconds of the rape attempt, she had broken his arm, his jaw, and rendered him unconscious on the ground. We feel such a training approach is far more useful to developing the capability to physically resist hostage situations than tournament fighting or forms competitions.

Remember!

Know your limitations.
Consider your fellow hostages.
Know when and if to use violence.
Wait for the right time.
Don't give away your true speed too early.
Be committed to your attack.
Be very aggressive.
Follow through your strikes and use multiple techniques.
Always attack vulnerable target points.
Use devastating techniques that will put him down and keep him down.
Always use a weapon whenever possible, even if it's your car.
Be very careful if he has a weapon.
Study at a school that can teach you practical martial arts.

[1] Robert K. Spear, *Hapkido: The Integrated Fighting Art*, Unique Publications, 4201 Vanowen Place, Burbank, CA, 91505, 1988.

See the information in the Resources section on the last page of this book to buy Bob's self-defense books, video tapes, and seminars.

CHAPTER 7

EXECUTING THE ESCAPE

One thing can be said for an escape you plan to execute, "It's either going to be successful or it's not." A very basic and blunt statement, yes, but in executing an escape, it's the only statement you can make with any certainty.

The chance for an escape may arise for which you did not plan. You may decide on the spur of the moment to take it. This, however, should be the exception. As stated earlier, once you have decided that an escape attempt is more advantageous than remaining in captivity, you must start to plan the escape. Sound planning will dramatically increase the odds that your escape will be successful.

The physical execution of the escape plan can be considered phase two of the escape execution. This phase is without a doubt the most critical phase to the escape. In this phase, even the slightest mistake can cost you your chance for freedom and, even more importantly, your life. [1] American hostage, Alann Steen, escaped from his captors but was spotted and turned in by neighbors in the Beirut, Lebanon suburb where he was being held. Released fellow hostage, Mithileshwar Singh, told US authorities that the 49-year-old Steen was beaten for the escape attempt by his captors until several fillings were knocked out of his teeth. He obviously chose the wrong time to make his getaway or he was unlucky. There are certain facets of an escape attempt; however, that if done correctly will place the odds in your favor so your escape attempt will be successful:

- Evaluate
- Develop Rapport
- Assess Routines
- Gut Check
- Confronting Confrontation
- Blend In
- Seek Help
- Travel
- Vehicle Uses

Evaluate

If you are satisfied that your physical and mental fitness states are adequate to assessment indicate that the captors have altered their routine, particularly by increasing or changing the guards, then you may need to rethink and reassess your chosen time and method for initiating the escape. Remember, changes in the normal routines of captors usually occur for some reason or purpose. They may have caught on that you are planning an escape. They may suspect a rescue operation. Beirut hostages, for example, are moved frequently because their captors fear a US rescue effort. Maybe they just decided to alter their routine to relieve their own boredom.

You will probably not know the reason and, therefore, you will have to reassess your captors and your situation to determine the impacts of the change(s) on your own plans. If, however, your assessment does reinforce your initial selection for an escape time and means, then you are ready to get serious.

Gut Check

You have a plan. You have developed rapport with your captors, and you have chosen and assessed a time and method of escape. Now it's time for a gut check — a last minute self-evaluation during which you must determine whether you have the will to do what must be done to escape and remain free. Look at the man, woman, boy, or girl who is guarding you and ask yourself, "Can I injure or more likely kill that person and maybe others?"

Your answer must not be based upon self-delusions! If you cannot answer, "yes," without reservation, you might want to rethink the whole operation. You must certainly be willing to face the alternatives to yourself when faced with a life-or-death situation. Once you have dealt with the ethics of your dilemma, you are ready to initiate your escape. Remember the guys on the ill-fated 9/11 flight who decided to take on their captors in an attempt to save many lives, sacrificing their own and their fellow passengers. They weighed the odds and decided to go for it. **Lets Roll!**

Confrontation

Unless you are extremely lucky, you will have to overpower a guard to get free initially. The physical confrontation required to overpower the guard must be initiated with no hesitation and finished quickly. Surprise is key! Any hesitation may give the guard a chance to resist and successfully defend himself while simultaneously injuring or killing you. It could also result in a prolonged confrontation providing time for other captors to discover the escape attempt and then intercede.

The results of such a confrontation should be your initial freedom and the inability of the guard to scream for help or to physically pursue you. Such desired results will usually mean rendering the guard unconscious or dead. Lets face it, you are not going to have time to practice knot tying and the time it will take to tie up the guard is time that you could be using to get away. As stated earlier, hopefully you have already made a "gut check". One point to consider, if you kill the guard and are captured later, your captors might decide to give you the same treatment. Given an option, Mike Moak suggests trying to leave the guard unconscious.

Initial Freedom

Once initially free, the average escapee will feel both excitement and fear: excitement at finally being free and fear of the unknown. The key is to control your emotions while remaining flexible in your actions.

As you move from your initial place of captivity, you may experience other guards or lookouts. If you are undetected and there are avenues of escape, use them by all means. If there is no other way out and/or if you are detected, then once again you must decide what actions you are willing to take. If the situation allows you to successfully overcome the guard(s), then do so.

Blend In

Once clear of the initial site of your captivity, there will be certain actions you must take. First, if you are in a foreign country, you must blend into your surroundings until you can find reliable help. The optimum method is to have on clothing, which is native to the area. If you don't have such clothing, continue to move within the crowds until you are safely away from your initial captivity site. Once safely away, you can acquire native dress by stealing it off of clothes lines.

If you leave the area of confinement carrying a weapon, don't throw it away and don't carry it in the open while moving within crowds of people. To do so would be like carrying a sign saying, "Here I am." Conceal it somewhere on your person. On the other hand, if you are escaping a criminal hostage situation and the confinement area is surrounded by the police, drop the weapon as soon as you get clear, so that you are not shot by mistake.

Seek Help

If during your movement you spot friendly police or military officials, move quickly but calmly to their location and seek their help. If you were held hostage in your own country, reporting to such officials will most likely end your ordeal. This is probably also your best alternative in a foreign country, particularly if you are lost and have no idea where or who else to go to. Be careful however! In some countries, the police are no better than and, in some cases, support those who kidnap foreigners. If you feel this is your situation, it might be wiser to get further away and attempt to locate a business, consulate, embassy, or church sect, which you know to be friendly to your native country. Such organizations or agencies will probably be more than happy to provide sanctuary but, because of their location and situation, they must be careful in how they support you. While you are free, this may still mean a long stay in a concealed location until friendly powers can be brought to bear on your situation. The Canadian Embassy personnel courageously hid several American Embassy personnel for months during the Iranian takeover and later were able to spirit them away. Had their support been discovered, they may have suffered the same fate as our people did.

Travel

Upon getting away from your confinement area, you may

have to travel some distance to ensure your getaway is successful. While, as stated previously, this will probably not be necessary if you are in your native country, it is almost a foregone conclusion in other places such as Beirut, Lebanon. In Beirut, an escaped hostage would probably have to travel many kilometers down back alleys and through rundown neighborhoods to escape not only the area in which he was held but also the entire community or section of the city that identifies with his prior captors' cause.

Such a journey may require you to travel by night and to rest in out-of-the-way places like sewers, abandoned buildings, under bridges, and in garbage dumpsters. Night travel is more secure but it also affords you less opportunity to find open an organization or agency, which is friendly to your native country. It also reduces your observation and the size of crowds, which could cover your movement. Daylight, on the other hand, provides much larger crowds for you to blend in with around an urban environment, but pursuers can find you easier. Without knowing any more details about Alann Steen's escape attempt, we can only surmise that he made his break during the daylight which made him easier to spot. A good compromise might be to travel by night, rest by day, and attempt contact with friendly groups right after opening or right before closing hours.

To maintain your strength and stamina during your flight to freedom, you may have to steal food or eat out of the garbage just to survive. Such a means to an end is justified when that end is freedom and safety.

Vehicle Uses

The option to traveling by foot upon your initial escape is to travel by vehicle or animal. The use of a vehicle, most likely stolen, to further your escape offers you speed, increased security, and, if need be, a weapon. A vehicle will function quite nicely as an expedient weapon, if a hostile foot or vehicle patrol blocks your way. Just remember, once you decide to ram a blockade or patrol, floor it and go. As we have stated before, hesitation could be your undoing.

The negative aspect of using a vehicle to continue your escape is that traffic sometimes moves slowly. You are apt to be spotted as a foreigner and quickly identified by those loyal to your former captors.

A second issue you should assess, when considering the

use of a car for your getaway, is one we discussed earlier. How friendly are the local police? If they are friendly to your country, there's no problem. Simply drive around until you see one and drive right up to him. If, on the other hand, the police are apt to favor your former captors, then it is not too smart to use a vehicle. One small traffic violation could cause you to be stopped by the police and ultimately result in your being returned to captivity. Given the trade-offs, however, we suggest using a vehicle at least initially to rapidly clear the area of your former captors.

Conclusions

Executing an escape attempt should not be taken lightly or done out of sheer frustration of being held hostage. Lack of detailed planning and situational assessment right up to the point where you actually execute the escape attempt will most likely result in failure and/or death. The decision to attempt an escape must be based upon whether your chances for survival are greater if you try to escape than if you remain in your present captivity.

Once you have decided that escaping your present situation is the best alternative, remember; plan your escape in detail. Given time, and you'll probably have lots of that, make your plan and evaluate it. Assess your captors and attempt to develop rapport with them. It is extremely important to gain as much of their trust as you can. Continue to reevaluate your plan and gain their trust.

Just as important as evaluating and reevaluating your plan is your honest evaluation of yourself. Make sure that you can do what must be done when and if the opportunity to escape presents itself. If you don't think you can intentionally injure or kill one or more of your captors, don't even try to escape if confrontation is likely since your captors will have no reservations about injuring or killing you.

If you think you have what it takes and you execute an initially successful escape, don't stop and congratulate yourself. Keep moving! Get as far away from where you were held captive as you can. Do everything you can to blend in with your surroundings. Assess your situation constantly to determine what time of day or night is best for movement, where you are and which way you should go. The key is to SURVIVE! Steal food and/or clothes if you must to survive. Do what you have to do.

Finally, attempt to find those you think can help you attain that ultimate objective you identified when you planned your escape. Ultimately, and particularly if you cannot find legal organizations (police, military, consulates, or embassies), you may have to trust someone to aid your escape unless you are planning to conduct an escape-and-evasion operation completely out of the state or country you are in. Again, this will be a difficult decision.

From the initial decision to escape, the selection of an escape plan, and the execution of the plan to freedom as your final objective, you must be extremely flexible to make numerous decisions. Executing an escape won't be easy, but if the option is torture or possibly death at the hands of your captors, there is no other alternative.

[1] AP New York Bureau story, *Stars and Stripes Newspaper*, 22 Nov, 88, P.2.

CHAPTER 8

RESCUE — WHO AND WHAT TO EXPECT

[1] On 28 June, 1981 at 10:55 a.m., Morris E. Roberts, Jr. gained entry to the Federal Building in Atlanta, Georgia. Through a series of events, he seized nine hostages and held them in the building's 10th floor FBI offices. At 1:37 p.m., Roberts released three of the hostages. Unbeknownst to Roberts and the remaining hostages, a rescue force of FBI SWAT and Atlanta Police Department personnel had gained access from the building's roof to a 10th floor mechanical maintenance room. From there they moved to a position behind a louvered wall vent. This observation post gave a view of Roberts and his hostages while concealing the observers from his view.

A little after 2:00 p.m., Roberts allowed all of his hostages to go to the bathroom at one time. He lined them up in a single file placing himself at the end of the file so that he could observe all the hostages as they moved toward the bathroom.

At 2:23 p.m., Roberts, while escorting the hostages back from the bathroom at gun point, passed by the louvered vent. As he passed by, Roberts was shot 42 times by the rescue force. He died without firing a shot.

A true story, this is an example of a well-planned and executed external force rescue of hostages. Not one hostage was injured during the rescue.

If you are taken hostage, the authorities will be looking for you! If they find you, they will do everything in their power to obtain your safe release. There are numerous types of rescue forces constantly training for the mission of hostage rescue. Most major countries have a national, usually military, force specializing in hostage release missions. The United States has a number of special military units, which are well-versed in all methods of hostage rescues. The US also has another well-trained national force, the FBI's Hostage Rescue/SWAT forces.

England has a highly elite and proven force called the Special Air Service (SAS). The SAS is the rescue force that stormed the Iranian Embassy on 5 May, 1980, in London and freed nineteen hostages while killing five terrorists and wounding a sixth. This operation, like the FBI operation discussed before, was flawlessly executed. The only death of a hostage was the death of the Iranian Press Attache who was killed earlier by the terrorists in an attempt to force British authorities to give in to the terrorists' demands.

Germany also has an extremely professional counter-terrorist force called GSG9. This battle-tested force is unusual because it is an elite national police unit, rather than a military one. On 13 October, 1977, a West German Lufthansa airliner with 82 passengers and a crew of five was hijacked on its return flight from the Spanish island of Majorca to West Germany. The plane with four hijackers on board, ultimately landed at Mogadissu Airport in Somalia. After five days of negotiation and constant refusals by the hijackers to release any of the people held hostage, the GSG9 stormed the airplane killing three of the hijackers and capturing the fourth. All hostages were freed unharmed.

While the rescue forces described above are all at national levels, you should remember that professionally trained rescue teams can be found at state, county, and even city levels of government. Many major cities have well-trained and seasoned rescue forces due to the nature and levels of crime in these cities frequently resulting in hostage situations.

Rescue Attempt

Another type of rescue force that has worked in the past is the privately organized and trained rescue force. An excellent example of such a force was organized by Ross Perot, Chairman of the Board of Electronic Data Systems (EDS) and third party presidential candidate in the 1992 elections. On December 28, 1978, two EDS executives were illegally imprisoned in Iran by Iranian officials. While no charges were filed against the two executives, they were put in detention with bond set at $12,750,000. Initially placed in detention, the two were later moved to the maximum security Gasr prison in Tehran. When US State Department initiatives failed and the US Government proved unwilling to cause a major confrontation over two American while approximately 12,000 other US citizens remained in Iran, Ross Perot organized his own rescue force. Perot first hired retired Colonel Bull Simons, organizer of the failed Son Tay raid which had been intended to free American prisoners-of-war from the North Vietnamese Son Tay war camp. Simons was to plan and run the EDS rescue operation. Simon's rescue force consisted of nine men (8 Americans and 1 Iranian) including himself. Except for Simons, all worked for EDS. Since the two prisoners had visitation rights, members of the team were able to alert the two of the impending rescue attempt. The rescue plan as executed consisted of grabbing the two during a riot of revolutionaries, which was started by the Iranian member of the team. They quickly fled the prison area and traveled for days cross-country in four-wheel drive vehicles. The rescue force and former hostages reached Turkey and flew back to the United States.

You can see by the above examples that rescue forces can vary in legality, organization, training and support. With the exception of Ross Perot's private force, all the rescue forces discussed above are considered legally constituted forces in the eyes of International Law. All the forces, excepting Perot's, are well organized and trained full-time professionals. All the forces, including Perot's, had excellent financial support. Ross Perot's rescue force, however, had something the others did not — relative freedom. This force, because it was private, could basically go and come as it wanted with no requirement to have any government's sanction.

The other important difference among the hostage rescue operations discussed previously was the difference in the situations:

- One was a criminal, single-captor with nine hostages in an office building.
- The second involved storming an embassy which was a very large building with many places for terrorists to hide and hold hostages.
- The third consisted of a small physical structure, an air liner, jammed with passengers and crewmembers who had no place to run or hide once the shooting started.
- And finally, one consisted of a situation which required going into the "Enemy's" country, working clandestinely without government support where the rescue force was greatly outnumbered and outgunned.

Yet, with all the differences, each of the above rescue operations was successful. This should give you some sense of security and satisfaction knowing if you are taken hostage, your chances are good that a rescue force can free you unharmed. And, if you are taken hostage, what can you expect of a rescue force that may be invisible to you and your captors until the last second? Let's take a look.

Intelligence Operations

Once the authorities have learned of your abduction, they will initiate intelligence operations to gain information about your abduction as quickly as possible. Since timing is critical, the authorities will want to gather as much information as they can before any leads begin cooling off. They will want to act quickly to negate your captors' moves to transport you or reinforce their defenses with more people, weapons, or booby-trapped explosive charges around the holding area. The specific information they will be seeking can be broken down into three areas:

- the hostages,
- the hostage takers,
- and the hostage-holding location.

The Hostages

The authorities will attempt to determine the following information as a minimum:

- Who you are.
- What you look like.
- What is your general mental and physical condition?
- Is there any particular reason why you were taken hos tage instead of someone else?

You may ask, "Why are the authorities trying to get so much information on me? I'm the good guy!" The answer is that the rescue force will want to know as much about you as they can. Such information as knowing you are ill or wounded and require medical treatment may help win your release or provide a means of infiltrating the physical structure where you are being held by a rescue force member posing as a doctor. Such an infiltration could gain vital the physical structure where you are being held by a rescue force member posing as a doctor. Such an infiltration could gain vital information about your abductors and/or their defenses. Knowing what you look like would be critically important if the rescue force must assault the holding location. Such information would greatly decrease the chances of you being shot by mistake by the rescue force during an assault. Knowing if there was a reason for your abduction might help a hostage negotiator in his attempt to win your release and in calming your captors.

The Hostage Takers

Information that can be gathered on your abductors will be extremely critical to any hostage negotiations or assault plans. Similar to the hostages, knowing how many bad guys are involved, their roles, and what they look like, is crucial. Knowing the intentions and motives of the hostage takers is essential to understanding them and the situation. Are they revolutionaries who have specifically targeted you? Are they criminals with a personal profit motive? Are they criminals who happened to grab you as a convenient target of opportunity for their security? Such information will be vitally important to a hostage negotiator who is trying to win your freedom and save your life. If your abductors are in fact members of some revolutionary/terrorist organization and you are being held in a location controlled by those who support their cause, this information is vital to the rescue force that may have to enter that area to free you. Knowing that your abductors are in fact members of some group may also, through research of the group's prior actions, help the authorities determine what your abductors are likely to do during the situation.

Finally, it is extremely important to know what types of weapon systems and explosives the bad guys are likely to have, since it is essential to the rescue force's assault plan.

Knowing something about the hostage takers will greatly increase predictability of their probable actions and responses.

The Hostage-Holding Area

Probably the most important piece of information that authorities need in a hostage situation is the exact location of the hostages. If the authorities don't know where you are, they can't come and get you. This has been the major problem in Lebanon. Trying to find the exact locations of all the Americans being held has been the major stumbling block in any attempt to launch a rescue force. This was true in the Iranian hostage situation, in the Vietnam War POW holding, and would be a real problem in Iraq.

Once the authorities find out where you are being held, they can then intensify their collection efforts to determine the inner structure (hidden ceilings, elevator shafts, air conditioning ducts, room layouts, etc.) of the site. They will also try to ascertain what types of communications your abductors have and how well stocked they are with supplies.

The next most critical information items they must gather are your exact position within the holding structure and the nature of your abductors' defenses between your location and the rescue force.

Securing the Site

Once intelligence operations have determined at least where you are being held hostage, the next step in gaining your freedom is to secure and cordon off the area so your captors can't move you or get away themselves. Securing a hostage site can be easily done in a place such as New York City or London. Such an action allows authorities to gain some control over the situation from which they can begin other actions such as hostage negotiations, detailed reconnaissance, or planning and launching a rescue attempt. You may not know that the area has been cordoned off and secured. Your abductors might not know either, initially, until they have been contacted or try to move.

Once they know, your abductors may or may not tell you. If you notice that your captors are acting strangely, especially after receiving a phone call and/or cease leaving the holding area, you may want to start mentally rehearsing your abductor release or your external-rescue-force plans in case negotiations are successful or a rescue assault is attempted. Sometimes hostages will know the area is secured by a friendly force due to the hostage negotiator, once he has established contact with the captors, asking often to talk to a hostage to determine the condition of him or any other hostage.

If you are told to talk to a hostage negotiator, remain calm and do exactly as your abductor tells you to. He has at least allowed you to make contact with those who are seeking your freedom, so stay calm and follow instructions. If you do, the hostage negotiator may be able to talk your abductor into releasing you. As stated previously, securing an area in New York or London can be done very easily and such an action allows for further planning on the spot. In a hostile location such as Lebanon or other unfriendly area, the securing of the area around the holding-site will have to occur immediately prior to or simultaneously with a rescue attempt. This means that you should plan for a rescue attempt early on in your captivity.

Hostage Negotiations and Other Actions

The primary objective in any rescue operation is the safe release of the hostages and the protection of lives (hostages, rescue force, and bystanders). Because of this and prior to an assault being mounted to free the hostages, a hostage negotiator will be brought in attempting to persuade the abductors to release the hostages unharmed and to give up. Normally the person brought in to conduct the negotiations is highly trained, having learned his skills through both experience and study. He possesses stamina and confidence, which is critical for the effort he must undertake.

Quite often, hostage negotiators are very successful. One of the first things the negotiator will do is ask to speak with the hostage. Do exactly what your abductor tells you while you compose yourself to talk with the negotiator. Remember, the only reason you are talking to the negotiator at all is because the negotiator has persuaded your abductors to allow this. So play along, let the negotiator handle the situation. While talking to the negotiator, especially over the phone, be prepared to answer questions. Don't get emotional! Neither you nor the negotiator needs this added stress and the abductors may stop the conversation early.

If the hostage negotiator does persuade your abductors to release you, GO! Do exactly as your abductors tell you but don't hesitate or worry about belongings you may have and want to take along. The only important thing you should be concerned with is getting out alive. If you are one of many hostages and freedom for only some of you has been arranged, don't argue over why some are going free and others are staying, just allow those chosen to go free. Again remember, the hostages are going because a negotiator has obtained their freedom from the abductors. Don't hinder his progress! To those left behind, think positively! Negotiations are working, play along!

Quite often a hostage negotiator can do no more than initially buy time. This time, however, is time rescue force personnel can use to plan assaults, conduct detailed reconnaissance, and infiltrate into the holding site. The key point you need to remember is that you have a vital role to play during the hostage negotiations. Short of harming someone, do whatever your captors and the hostage negotiator tell you to do.

The Assault

The last thing you probably ever wanted to be is a hostage; even worse, a hostage during a rescue force assault. A rescue attempt will be made when hostage negotiations have broken off completely, when the authorities believe you are in danger of being harmed, or you are being held in a hostile location such as Lebanon where no one is interested in negotiating.

You will probably not even know the rescue force is in position until they begin the assault to free you. Normally the rescue force will consist of an assault force (the force coming in to get you) and a support force (the force which provides covering fire and any needed distractions).

Rescue — Who and What to Expect

The rescue force will normally move as close to the location where you are being held as possible while remaining out of sight. They will form an assembly area, where they will make final coordination and planning based on all intelligence provided. Individuals will be assigned specific responsibilities. Routes (hopefully concealed) to the location where you are being held will be selected as will exact points of entry into the location. Methods for the physical penetration of the site such as explosives, pry bars, ramming devices, or rapelling ropes will be chosen.

Procedures for clearing every room and for rapidly securing and removing hostages will also be determined. Planning for the assault will continue until the order is given to commence the attack.

Once the order is given to the rescue force commander to free you, the rescue force will commence a quiet, well-concealed, and disciplined movement into the location where you are being held. The support team will cover the flanks and rear of the site and will position snipers to provide covering fire as needed. The assault team will move in as closely as possible and then execute the penetration.

Your first indications of a rescue attempt may be a wall being blown down or a huge hole suddenly appearing in the ceiling/floor of the room where you're being held. From out of the hole may appear people dressed like Martian troopers- they might have on night-vision goggles, gas masks, and flak vests. Don't jump up and you have not been too traumatized during your ordeal. If you have, they will try to identify follow-on treatment, counseling, and rehabilitation. The next thing you will probably go through is a thorough debriefing. This will be conducted by intelligence officials (local, state, or national, depending on who was holding you and who rescued you). They will be attempting to determine as much information about your abductors as they can. Support this debriefing completely since it may prove the basis for a future hostage rescue.

Conclusion

For many individuals held hostage, the only means of gaining freedom is through the actions of a rescue force. If you are taken hostage, you can be confident that the legal authorities are looking for you. Once they find you, they will do anything within their power to obtain your freedom. If the situation dictates that a hostage rescue force must free you, remember that most such forces are extremely professional. The rescue force will use detailed planning, speed, shock, and a coordinated effort to free you. For your part, develop a plan that keeps you as safe as possible during the assault. Remember, your initial warning that an assault is taking place may be a stunning explosion, or the captor standing next to you may suddenly fall dead to the floor from a sniper's bullet. Will you be ready to do the right actions? **Get down and out of the way!**

[1] *Terrorism Counteraction* A823, 1985/86, Atlanta Georgia FBI File Case.

CHAPTER 9

GETTING BACK TO NORMAL

Let's say you have been taken hostage and have been fortunate enough to be released, to escape, or to be rescued. How will you feel? What do you need to watch out for? What should you do?

Remember how a common reaction to being taken hostage is an initial sense of disbelief, as if this couldn't be happening to you. Now that it has happened, you may feel, "This really did happen to me. I'm now different than I was. Why doesn't everybody else realize that?"

We feel this reaction is similar to that experienced by many Vietnam veterans when they initially came back home. In their case, one day they were fighting in the jungle and heat, watching their buddies die and experiencing the mind-numbing terror of combat. The next day they found themselves strolling down their hometown main street.

They had a very deep sense of unreal feelings that none of their old acquaintances would ever truly understand them again. When a car backfired, they may have automatically dived to the ground with their combat survival reactions still in place.

As it was for the war veteran, so it can be with ex-hostages. A direct correlation can even be made with the pervasiveness and long lasting effects these experiences often have. Just as there are some Vietnam veterans who still find it difficult to deal with their past war experiences twenty years and more later, the ex-hostage may also find his terror and trauma lingering on. Even though the captivity experience may have only lasted a few hours, the aftereffects may hang on for years. Let's take a look at some of these post-incident reactions and what can be done to return to a life of normalcy.

The Stockholm Syndrome Revisited

As mentioned before, it is common to become emotionally attached to the hostage taker during the incident. It is also common to fear or become angry with the negotiating authorities and rescuers because they are perceived as life-threatening to the hostage. After the incident is over, it is not uncommon to feel guilt, shame, and puzzlement over these feelings. Indeed, these post-incident reactions are so common that they have become known as the fourth phase of the Stockholm syndrome.

Common Problems

There are a number of problems that frequently occur after the hostage incident is over. Some of these are physical in nature:

- Loss of appetite
- Unexplainable episodes of dizziness
- Sexual dysfunctions
- Sleep disturbances and insomnia

Many of the problems; however, are psychological:

- Being startled easily
- Shame and guilt
- Decreased motivation
- Claustrophobia and other phobias
- Anxiety caused by decision-making
- An erratic or changing temperament
- Nightmares and recurring dreams of the incident
- A feeling of being cheated out of life experiences
- A feeling of numbness or detachment

- A sense of entitlement
- Withdrawing from former interests and relationships
- Difficulties in memory or concentration
- Avoidance of "Triggers"
- Unwillingness to be "Treated" by a counselor

Physical Problems

Physical problems arising from the stress of captivity may last a few days or a few years. Sometimes they never go away. They may be further complicated if torture or physical deprivation was involved during the captivity period. In the first case, these physical problems are a manifestation of psychological problems. In the second case, injuries and degraded health are the problem. Together, they produce a rather poor physical condition. This is why it is best to be in excellent shape before becoming involved in a hostage situation. POWs who have survived the best are usually those who started out without injury or illness and were fit. If you are in a high-hostage-risk profession, you should participate in a regular physical conditioning program just in case you find yourself unexpectedly in a hostage situation.

Psychological Problems

The psychological aftereffects of being a hostage are on many occasions, much more harmful and longer lasting than the physical ones. Professional therapists have a term for these effects: 1 **post-traumatic stress disorder**. Its effects are dangerous because its symptoms will often mix with preexisting problems not previously diagnosed. The counselor is then presented with the challenge of determining which symptom was caused by the hostage experience and which one may have existed before. The therapist has to be very careful to determine what caused which symptoms and how to treat them properly.

2 "The experience of the terrorist's victim is highly unique and replicated by few other situations in life. Captivity may be only a few hours but can last for days or years. Very few people ever expect to become the victim of terrorists (editor's note — these statements can be applied equally to any hostage taker and not just to terrorists). Particularly devastating for victims is the role of a pawn in a drama beyond their control and frequently beyond their comprehension. The victim perceives himself or herself as valueless and debased. Not infrequently the terrorist incident involves unfamiliar issues that further contribute to the victim's bewilderment. When demands seem outrageous and unmeetable and the victim's life is at stake, helplessness is suffused with panic.

Often, the hostage develops a bond with the terrorist in which the latter is perceived as the protector — the so-called Stockholm syndrome...... Paradoxically, the authorities are viewed as the dreaded enemy. For the victim, the bond serves a defensive function, mitigating fear and helplessness. Following the incident, however, it may become a source of guilt that threatens to disrupt later treatment interventions."

The psychological disturbances left as an aftermath to this experience are varied and are often found as multiple rather than single symptoms.

Startle Response

Psychologists describe this phenomenon as an exaggerated startle response, we call it being jumpy. If you find yourself overreacting to sudden noises, lights, or movements, by jerking or jumping, you have this symptom. It's basically the fight-or-flight instinct operating. If you've been a hostage victim, you've been programmed by the situation to be overly sensitive to your environment. This will pass as you gain confidence that you are no longer in direct danger.

Shame and Guilt

It's not uncommon to feel shame in allowing oneself to be captured as a hostage or being instrumental in allowing others to become taken. This is especially true if personal carelessness played a roll in the beginning of the incident. For instance, a security guard answers a knock on the back door of a bank by opening it before checking to see who is knocking thereby allowing bank robbers into the bank. If they then take hostages, he might condemn his own careless action for years.

A hostage may have been released early. He might feel guilty that he suffered less than hostages who may have been kept longer. This is especially common if any of those other hostages were injured or killed. He'll wonder if he could have prevented their harm or if he was less worthy than those killed. It's very important to tell the ex-hostage it's OK to have survived!

Decreased Motivation

A hostage incident forces one into submissiveness. This can transfer over into post-incident reality and cause the victim to lose a zest for life. His fear to do anything that might cause harm keeps him from doing anything of meaning once he has been released.

Claustrophobia and Other Phobias

Captivity may cause a fear of confinement in small spaces or in crowds. If that confinement has been for a very long period; however, the victim may become agoraphobic, afraid of wide open spaces. This is seen from time to time in long-term convicts.

All sorts of other fear obsessions may be triggered if not directly caused by the incident.

Decision Making Anxiety

Both the hostage takers and the outside authorities constantly urge the hostage to take no action on his own, to sit back and allow the drama to play itself out. Is it any wonder some people find it difficult to make their own decisions after their life depended upon being passive?

Temperament

An erratic or changing temperament means that one has become emotionally unbalanced by the uncertainty of living brought about by being a hostage. Basically the emotions have been overloaded with stress. Now the victim is not sure of the emotional rules for reacting to stimulus and the environment.

Dreams

Nightmares and recurring dreams are very common. To this day, some of the Tehran Embassy hostages have bad dreams about being followed by their ex-captors even in America. This is the mind's way of dealing with a negative experience. You might even relive certain scenes from the incident over and over in your dreams. Again, this is a normal mind-coping mechanism. This is a very close parallel to veterans reliving their wartime experiences. A good therapist may be able to find the cause of these dreams and help you to work through them until emotional balance, stability, and security is reattained.

Missing Life Experiences

If you're held captive long enough, you may miss the birth of a child or an important milestone in his or her life. You might miss baptisms, anniversaries, birthdays, graduations, a baby's first step, a job opportunity, or the death of a loved one. It would be natural to feel like you've been cheated out of important parts of life. This can create of resentment toward anyone having anything to do with your capture, your captivity, and especially in prolonging your captivity.

Detachment

Forced submissiveness, shock, and helplessness can cause you to become numb or detached from reality. This is closely related to a lack of motivation and decision anxiety. It was safer to tune out during the stress of the incident and that has carried over to later daily life. It becomes an automatic response to any and all stress stimuli.

Post Traumatic Stress Disorder expert, Dr. Aphrodite Matsakis, neatly summarizes this condition in her excellent book, "Vietnam Wives", which is about Vietnam veteran PTSD and its effect on families.

[3] "Psychic or emotional numbing is a natural and normal human response to being relatively helpless in a situation of great danger. In order to cope with the crisis, the individual tends to shut down emotionally and focus all his attention on surviving. Problems arise when the emotional numbing lasts beyond that needed for survival or is extended to situations which are not life threatening.

Numbing almost always causes havoc and misunderstandings in marriage and other relationships requiring the expression of deep feelings. The veteran's difficulties in feeling his feelings, his fear of loss, and his fear of emotional pain often prevent him from establishing an emotionally close relationship with his wife. In some cases, the vet's numbing alternates with periods of emotional openness. In other cases, he may shun emotional relationships with women entirely or be able to relate to his wife on only a very limited basis.

The veteran's wife may interpret her husband's coldness as a personal rejection. As a result, she may build her own defenses against the veteran, have low esteem, and become numb to her own emotions, just like her husband. The vet's wall is a formidable barrier to marital communication, leaving the wife feeling shut out and alone."

The ex-hostage needs to be reminded that it's OK to have feelings and emotions and to let them out!

A Sense of Entitlement

Many come away from their captivity thinking, "Look

what I just went through! Somebody owes me for this!" Many victims feel that they should receive free medical treatment, that the government should recompense them for their poor treatment, that their company should pay them a reward because it put them in harm's way, that their family should be paid for their anxiety while waiting to see if the hostage was going to come through safely.

Withdrawal

Again, this is closely related to other "dropout" coping mechanisms. You may feel, "I'm no longer the same; therefore, I can no longer remain in this relationship since we have nothing in common anymore," or "It's dangerous and uncomfortable to have emotions; therefore, I must not let myself become too involved with life," or "It's dangerous out there, I might get taken again."

Degradation of Mental Skills

Victims will often have difficulties with their memory and concentration. This also is typical of emotional overload. It's as if the stress of the situation has blown out circuit paths and synapses in your brain. When you're trying to forget fear and pain, other things may be indiscriminately lost as well. It may be more difficult to concentrate on something if, deep down, you're afraid and that is interfering with your conscious thought processes.

Avoidance of "Triggers"

Many victims avoid painful memories of their experience. If they find that certain common everyday happenings cause them to relive that anguish, they will avoid these "Triggers".

[4] "Closed spaces, situations lacking ready access, or television programs depicting violence, even seemingly innocuous fare such as football games, are avoided since they arouse traumatic memories and feelings."

Unwillingness to be Treated

We Americans are terrible about always wanting to gut out everything. Often we feel it's not macho to seek counseling assistance. The hostage victim also has this to deal with. In addition, the resentment of authority figures transferring over from the Stockholm syndrome plus the guilt that maybe he did something wrong to have become a victim or in the way he acted while he was a victim cause him to resist badly needed help. This reluctance must be overcome! It is said that only one third to one half of ex-hostages who suffer from these symptoms ever seek help. They allow their fears from the incident and their concern others will think them crazy override their need for assistance.

Family Problems

Its not unusual for ex-hostages to find that they have family problems if their captivity has been a long one. If the family was not accustomed to being apart, the partner who was left behind had to cope with an expanded role. For instance, a mother might find herself as the head of the household, having to make decisions and to think about certain subjects with which she has little experience. When should the car's oil be changed? Who should do it? What should she do and say when Junior comes home from school crying because some bully beat him up or teased him? Just as disturbing is the father who is suddenly "Mr. Mom". What color should your daughter's prom dress be? What happens if your ten-year-old starts menstruating?

Any of these might be disturbing situations to someone not accustomed to dealing with them. It is even possible for the one left behind to feel resentful for being left holding the bag. Yet, often they cope and they do it very well. Herein lies the problem, the hostage comes home, recently traumatized, ready to move back into a family role, and what does he or she find? At least a portion of their duties have been usurped by their marriage partner who is now accustomed to doing them. Perhaps the rest of the family has become accustomed to the new arrangement and prefers it. Can you imagine how threatening that must feel to someone who has just spent a long time feeling helpless? Now the hostage is back, yet there still seems to be continuing feelings of frustration and helplessness exacerbating the emotional hangover from the hostage situation.

This is a rather common phenomenon in Service families who go through periodic separations. Role adjustment, sharing, letting go, and reestablishing happen relatively often in military families. What seems to help is having a support group to assist the family through tough adjustment and readjustment periods by just being there when help or a shoulder to cry on is needed. This is especially true if the support group or circle of friends has been through similar trials and shares these personal experiences with the family in need of emotional support and understanding.

Professional counseling is also useful and should not be shunned. Sometimes objectivity is essential to clear up the challenges of disturbed family relations. A family counselor is trained to provide this kind of support. Again, the military community has a long and successful track record with support programs of this kind, since they are accustomed to the need.

The important thing to remember is you will never be able to go back home in the sense that some things are bound to change. Home will not be exactly as you remembered it. Try not to fight the problem, work with it and talk things out.

What Helps?

After seeing all the physical and mental problems brought about by having been a hostage, you might wonder what's the use? Why go on living in misery? We think, however, that you are the one element in this equation that can really make the difference. You might have been helpless during the hostage situation, but once you're out of it, you have the right, the capability, and the responsibility to control your life and what goes on in it! What you do counts so make it meaningful! These are fine sounding words, but how does one go about recovering from the aftereffect of being a hostage?

First, you need to expect problems and be willing to meet them head on. No one ever said it would be easy. You must be willing to try to overcome any problem that rears its head. Don't allow yourself the luxury of remaining helpless after the incident. That would be a cop out!

Second, you'll need to talk out your feelings. See a properly trained therapist and heed the advice and help you are given!

[5] Dr. Matsakis has summarized of what proper PTSD therapy for the Vietnam vet should consist. We would like to paraphrase it for the victims of hostage situations since they are also suffering from PTSD:

- Helping the victim uncover the specific events in the hostage situation which he has been attempting to deny or which he has been unable to accept.

- Supporting him as he feels the feelings associated with these traumatic events.

- Helping him acquire a greater understanding of how his hostage experiences have affected his life in the present.

- Helping the victim find constructive uses for his hos tage experience.

Get back into a routine as quickly as possible. Routines are natural sedatives in a manner of speaking. Lets face it, if you've just come back from being a hostage, you've probably enjoyed about as much excitement as you can stand. Settle back down into the humdrum of day-to-day life. Use this as an anchor to reality.

Finally and most importantly, emphasize the positive. Try not to dwell on all the bad things that happened or may still be happening as aftereffect. Think rather of those things about yourself and others that have grown and matured from this experience. Remember, a sword must be tempered in fire before it can become steel. So must we, as people, become inured to hardship so that we can grow and rise above the negative aspects of our captivity.

[1] Robert I. Simon, M.D. and Robert A. Blum, M.D., "After the Terrorist Incident: Psychotherapeutic Treatment of Former Hostages", *American Journal of Psychotherapy*, Vol. XLI, No 2, April 1987, P. 194.

[2] Ibid.

[3] Dr. Aphrodite Matsakis, *Vietnam Wives*, Woodbine House Inc., 1988, P. 48.

[4] Simon and Blum, P. 196.

[5] Matsakis, P. 274.

CHAPTER 10

HOW TO PREPARE THE FAMILY

Keys To Family Survival

Finding oneself in a developing hostage situation can be very upsetting. Imagine how much more anxiety would be generated if one's family is also involved. A hostage situation requires clear, concentrated thinking. The last thing needed is being distracted by worries for your spouse and children. The keys to improving your family's chances for survival are:

- speed
- instinctive actions
- discipline

If you must ram your car through a roadblock, for instance, you may not have the time to instruct your kids to get down or how to properly brace themselves. (It seems inevitable that one of the more stubborn little rascals is always ready to ask, "But why do we have to do that, Daddy?") Wouldn't it be nice if you had previously drilled them on what to do and they responded perfectly out of habit! If that sounds like a good idea to you, read on as we tell you how to prepare your family for the contingencies of hostage situations.

Family Training Session

Actually, the time to talk about emergency actions is long before the emergency takes place. In this chapter, we will discuss how to train your family for different contingencies. First, however, let us talk about the act of training itself. If you have young ones, its especially important to teach them and then reinforce the teaching several times. This does not mean you should spend some Saturday training them over and over for hours. Rather, you should do it once every day or so until they've learned what to do and then reinforce it thereafter in monthly training sessions lasting from fifteen to thirty minutes.

We try to present training approaches that use role-playing or fantasy plays so that the training is fun. If it's not fun, the children may not cooperate. Role-playing is also good for adults and teenagers since it allows the process of visualization, which is so important to mentally rehearsing one's actions for an emergency situation. The important thing is to allow your love for your family to shine through. Tell them the truth about why the family is playing some new games. Let them know that there are bad people in the world and that you want your family to stick together helping one another out in case bad people ever try to hurt them. Every action on the kids' part helps Mom or Dad do a better job of looking out for everyone. Tell them that if they learn to play these games well, they'll be ready should someone ever try to hurt the family.

HOSTAGE SITUATIONS IN THE HOME

Regardless of how many precautions one takes, if someone really wants to kidnap a person, they can usually find a way. General Dozier knew that he had been targeted before his capture, yet he still let terrorists posing as maintenance men into his apartment. What if there had been small children there? This first game is designed for a contingency where someone (terrorist or criminal) is trying to break into your dwelling.

RED LIGHT GAME

Dad or Mom yells out "Red Light" or some other innocuous key phrase. Everyone else quickly and quietly runs to his or her pre-selected hiding place. Parents should go around the house with each child and help select personal places of safety: under a bed, in a toy chest, in a closet behind some clothes, or wherever. Since speed and silence are essential, the hiding place must readily accessible and provide enough concealment to escape a cursory search. They should practice being quiet until they hear the parent give the all clear "Green Light" signal. If they have to go "potty", tell them that it would be OK to go in their pants before they should break security and come out in a real-life situation. In the meantime, the parent who yelled "Red Light" should try to convince the abductors that they are alone.

If the parent is taken away, have the kids wait "a long time", come out slowly and very quietly, and then phone or run for help. They should know who to contact and alternative sources of help if the first party is unavailable. Let your neighbors or relatives know if they have been selected as a source of help. Tape the phone numbers for these contact people to the telephone so they are readily accessible to the children.

When you play the game, see how quickly and quietly they can hide. Talk through (role play) their self-release situations. The key here is for them to be ultra cautious.

The Safe Room

A possible alternative to the "Red Light" game is for all the family to instantly rush to a single, well-protected location in the house called a "Safe Room". This is much more effective than trying to play hide-and-seek with potential abductors; however, it is quite a bit more expensive. The Safe Room consists of an area lined with strong sheet steel (sides, top, and bottom) or reinforced concrete with a thick steel door. The room should be self-sufficient and may include a separate source of potable water, food supplies (Bob's family keeps 6-12 months on hand at all times), heat, cooling, electricity and/or lanterns, a port-a-potty, a separate phone with an unlisted number, or better yet, a police radio to advise the authorities that you are under attack. You should have a very loud alarm, which is audible all over the neighborhood to alert your neighbors to danger.

You should also keep a weapon and ammunition in the room just in case the attackers manage to break in. We recommend a 12-gauge shotgun with #4 Buck (which provides a wider pattern than double-ought buckshot). The ideal room would even be hermetically sealed with a separate source of air to preclude chemical/gas attacks. Its entrance should be situated in a narrow hallway so that it would be impossible to use a battering ram against the door, which can be readily barred by strong, steel bars and locked.

This may sound a little extreme; however, if you are wealthy or a highly probable target for abduction or assassination attempts, it might be a worthwhile investment. Both authors know of people who really do go to such lengths to protect themselves and their loved ones. An old bomb shelter from the fifties' nuclear paranoia might suit one's security needs very well. Such a room is quicker to get to by all the family and far more secure than trying to hide in or around the house.

Suspicious Mail

Although not a hostage threat, suspicious mail fits into the category of those things that "bad people" do and is something your family should be trained to detect. The advent of plastique explosives, which are very powerful and easily molded into thin sheets, brings a special threat to those highly visible people who may become targets of terrorists or crazies. Using plastique and flat batteries such as found in Polaroid cameras, these people could construct letter bombs capable of killing or maiming.

SAFE ROOM

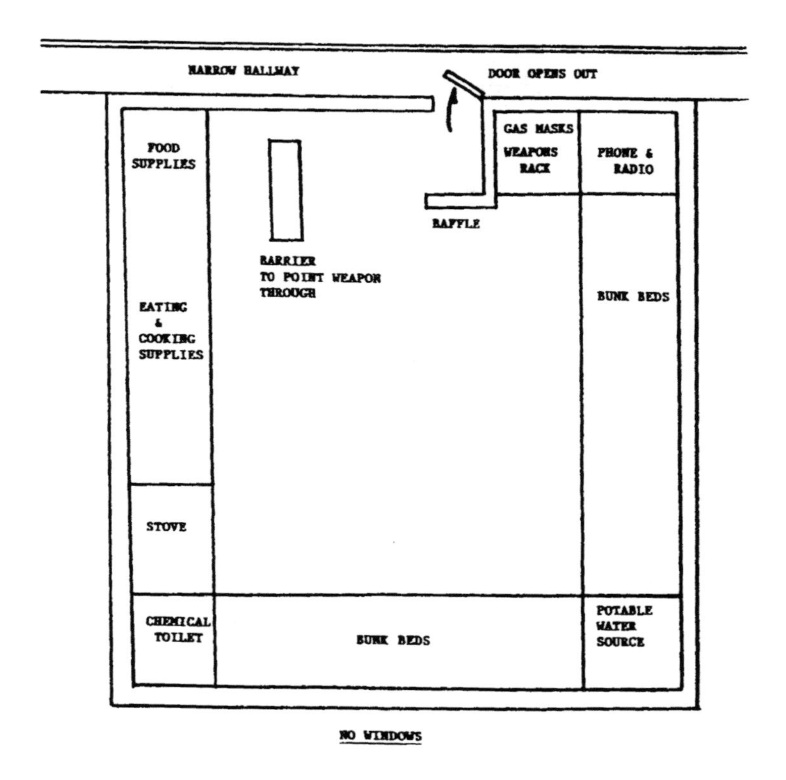

Explosives aren't the only threat. The movie, "Cry for Freedom", a reenactment of a white liberal newspaper editor's involvement in the South African antiapartheid struggle, depicts this danger quite well. The editor's family received a package with no return address containing T-shirts depicting the picture of a Black South African leader. As the children excitedly began to pull the shirts over their heads, they started screaming violently. The shirts had been laced with a strong powdery acid, which severely burned the children's' faces and shoulders. Pro-apartheid forces had sent the package as a warning to the family that their involvement in the Blacks' struggle for freedom was not appreciated.

In your training sessions, tell your family to never handle mail that:

- Has no return address or stamp.
- The person or firm indicated on the return address is

Typical Suspicious Mail

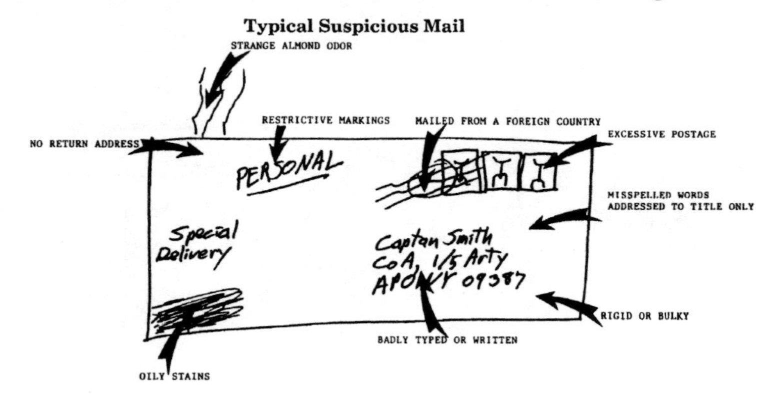

not recognizable or known.

- The name and address are composed of letters clipped from magazines or newspapers.
- Many of the names or words are misspelled.

In order to teach your family how a letter bomb might appear, roll out some "silly-putty" or "play dough" into a sheet that will fit into an envelope. Scent the putty with almond extract. Use butter or grease to make some stains on the envelope. If you have a Polaroid flat battery, put it into the envelope too. A small round pillbox will make a good firing device replica. You now have a training aid that has the same feel, heft, smell, and appearance as a letter bomb would have.

Handling Phone Calls and Answering the Door

Don't allow would-be kidnappers easy access into your home and don't allow them to conduct a reconnaissance by telephone. Teach your family members good home security methods. For instance, if a stranger calls on the phone and asks your child whether Daddy is at home, your child should try to get the caller's name first. Then the child should call for Daddy or

Mommy. If neither is at home, the child then says, " Daddy or Mommy can't come to the phone right now," (perhaps they are in the bathroom or the bedroom, we'll let the caller fill in those possibilities in his own mind).

The child then asks if the parent can call back. This implies that the parent(s) are home and will get back to the caller whenever they are more conveniently disposed. Most importantly, it lends the appearance that there is at least a parent to protect the children in an emergency. It may also intimidate a would be kidnapper to have a kid interrogate him for his name. If the caller is legitimate, you can call him back to see if he really did call.

The same idea goes for answering the door. Make strangers identify themselves to your satisfaction before allowing them entry. If the visitor claims to be a repairman, ask to see his identification through the door's peep hole and check it out with his company by phone to see if he works for them and if in fact they sent him. If he says he's from the phone company and he needs to get in to fix your phone, ask yourself these questions:

- How does he know whether your phone is dead or not?
- Is your phone still working?
- If your phone is dead, ask him to come back another time. Check him out after he's gone. He could have cut your phone line on the outside as a ploy to gain entry and to keep you from calling for help.

If the person at the door asks your child if his parents are home and they aren't, have your child treat the situation just like a phone call with a, "Daddy can't come to the door right now. Can I tell him who you are and he will get back with you?"

Teaching your family to handle strangers in this fashion will prevent potential kidnappers from taking advantage of parental absences.

Training for Situations in the Car

Emergencies while driving usually happen suddenly. This next game is excellent conditioning for both attempted kidnapping situations as well as traffic accidents that require the parent driving to give his or her full attention to handling the car.

The key word and game's name is "CRASH". When the parent (or anyone who spots a developing danger) yells "CRASH!", all the passengers should immediately bend down and grab their knees or ankles and stay that way until the all clear signal is given. This action does four things:

- It lowers most of the occupants' bodies below the win dow-line which reduces flying glass injuries.
- It braces the passengers more properly for multiple im pacts.
- It gets their heads down and out of the way in case the car rolls and the roof is crushed in.

- And, it allows the driver to concentrate on his driving more fully.

This will help the driver if he or she has to ram through a barricade or a vehicle, or to drive around obstacles over rough terrain, or to control the car through the finale' of the crash. Everyone in the car should always keep their seat belts fastened and the doors locked for safety and to keep out unwanted hitchhikers such as terrorists or criminals trying to gain access in a kidnap attempt.

In Public Transportation

If a hostage situation arises in a bus, train, or airplane, your family should be taught to stay quiet, listen to what the hostage takers are saying, and obey the parents' instructions immediately. To better protect the children, Dad, or in his absence, Mom, should sit in an aisle seat with the kids in the middle or against the window.

Remember, the hostage taker is going to be keyed up during the initial phases so the children must be encouraged to remain quiet and as calm as possible.

In Public Buildings

Hostage situations in the more open areas of public buildings such as banks, transportation terminals, restaurants, etc., are more dangerous because of security guards. This could mean gunplay, so it is important for the family to get down and out of the way as quickly as possible. A good game to play helping enforce this action is "Down and Freeze!". If there are several children in your family, you could make this one competitive.

One of the parents says "Down and Freeze". EVERYONE falls down and stays there until released by the one who called the key phrase. Keep playing until only one is left. In addition to being fun, everyone gets a chance to hone survival actions.

This game and key phrase is also excellent for hostage rescue situations. It's important that all the hostages get down and stay down when a rescue force breaks in. The rescuers have only seconds to neutralize the abductors and prevent their retaliation against the victims. Getting your family down and in a prone position increases their safety and makes the rescuers' job easier.

On the Street

Several years ago, Bob's wife, Barbara, was visiting San Francisco with three of their children for a convention. A rather sleazy man came up to them on the street and asked Barb who she was and where she was going. Before she could tell him to get lost, the kids volunteered the information. He then asked what they were doing there and she replied, "We're waiting for my husband who will be coming back any minute now."

"But Mommy," said the eight year old daughter, "you know Daddy is in Arizona right now!"

Barb was so scared (and really peeved at the kids for being so open with a stranger) that she gathered them up, said goodbye to the man, and hurried off. Fortunately, the man didn't follow them. Needless to say, there was a detailed critique of the kids' actions when they reached safety.

Don't find yourself in a tight spot unnecessarily. Teach your children to not be too helpful if a stranger is talking to Mom or Dad. The kids must understand that if Mom or Dad seem to be lying or confused in their conversation with a stranger, there may be a very good reason.

Tell them to NEVER volunteer information or contradict something a parent says in public situations. It might give a potential attacker just enough information and encouragement to try something tragic.

What to Do if Mom and Dad Are Taken Hostage

If someone should take one or both of the parents hostage, life must go on for those left behind. The parents should write clear, easy-to-follow instructions of what to do in this situation. The military calls this a contingency plan. We have included a skeleton draft plan in the Appendix as a fill-in-the-blanks model for the reader to use. It should include such things as:

- The Chain of Command: Who's in charge and who takes care of the kids if one or both of the parents are gone. (Make sure this is coordinated with the respon sible party in advance and that the legal guardianship papers are drawn up!)

- Special Instructions For those things needed done around the house or, if you own your own business, those things needed done to insure its survival.

This last may well be a separately written contingency plan. For those things around the house needing attention such as what to do in the case of a frozen water pipe, how to light the furnace, or how to close up the home before going away, etc. is important because your loved ones may have to move in with a friend or a relative or they may have to be independent for the first time.

- Locations of Important Documents: Documents such as insurance policies, deeds, bank/savings account books, wills, and powers of attorney should be kept in a safe place where they can be easily accessed. A bank's safety deposit box might be less accessible than a family lawyer's files.

- Medical Information A list of any required medications would be very important as would information on any allergies. Other critical information would be medical insurance account numbers and forms, names and phone numbers of doctors, locations of medicaV shot records.

- Communications Key words or phrases can be arranged ahead of time to enable hostages to give clues as to their location or states of health or captivity or whether they are making statements under duress. These may be com municated in ransom notes, video or audio taped state ments.

Charles Glass, an American journalist kidnapped and held by Shi'ite Moslems in South Beirut, was forced to read a video taped statement to the effect that he was working for the CIA.

[1] "I read the statement in an American Southern accent, an oblique attempt to indicate I was in Beirut's southern suburbs. I also tried to get my crossed fingers into the picture frame as a clue that I did not mean what I was saying. I learned later that when my colleagues at ABC News showed the tape to my wife, she shocked them by laughing, 'He's acting,' she said."

If they had prearranged some key actions or phrases ahead of time, they would have communicated better, especially since they knew he was going into a high-risk area.

• Financial Concerns: If you have savings, investments, or assurance that your company will pay your salary, instructions pertaining to these aspects belong here. Some insurance companies provide policies for ransom payment and family sustainment in case of the policyholder's kidnapping. Governments and private companies now purchase policies to protect high-risk executives and workers stationed abroad. Wealthy individuals may also purchase these. For example, a landowner in E1 Salvador paid an annual premium of $750,000 for $5 million of insurance coverage.

[2] "The existence of a kidnap policy should be kept a closely guarded secret, because knowledge that a substantial policy is in force may serve as an incentive to terrorists (or criminals) to kidnap the policy holder, since they may reckon that payment of the ransom will be sure and swift. A second problem with kidnap insurance is that not all insurance companies pay automatically and some will attempt to negotiate the ransom downward, a process that may take several months or longer."

Don't shut the barn door after the horse has escaped. Make sure your family is prepared to face the contingencies of hostage situations by training them until they know what to expect and can react to your guidance and warnings instinctively. Don't put off writing a hostage contingency plan. Use the appendix in the back of this book right away as a guide for writing *your* plan.

[1] Charles Glass, "Kidnapped in Beirut", *The Readers' Digest*, April 1988, (condensed from Rolling Stone), P. 94.

[2] Neil C. Livingstone, *The War Against Terrorism*, D.C. Heath and Company, 1982, P. 228..

CHAPTER 11

RECOMMENDATIONS FOR SURVIVAL

Throughout this book we've mentioned specific things to know and do to survive a hostage situation safely. In this chapter, we would like to capstone these suggestions and add a few more from acknowledged expert sources. We especially want to thank unnamed Department of Defense sources and three civilians who, we feel, have contributed significantly in this field:

• New York Police Detective (Retired) Frank A. Boltz Jr., Mr. Hostage Cop himself. Mr. Boltz is a pioneer in the field of hostage negotiations and has written two fine books on the subject: [1] *Hostage Cop* and [2] *How to be a Hostage and Live.*

• Neal C. Livingston, author of the book, [3] *The War Against Terrorism,* is president of the Institute on Terrorism and Subnational Conflict and past director for terrorism and low-level warfare at the American Security Council in the Washington D.C. area. Neal and Bob have talked at several Soldier of Fortune conventions and have found themselves to agree on many aspects of this subject.

• Gayle Rivers, author of [4] *The War Against the Terrorists:*

How to Win It and several other related books. Mr. Rivers, a pseudonym, is purported to be a highly experienced mercenary. Whether he is real or not, we appreciate his philosophies and thought-provoking books.

We have organized specific recommendations into the different aspects and phases of usual hostage situations to include:

- Pre-Incident Preventative Security Measures.
- The Capture Phase.
- Transport and/or Consolidation Phase.
- The Confinement/Holding Phase.
- Physical Resistance.
- Psychological Resistance.
- Escape Planning and Execution.
- Incident Termination.
- Post Incident.

Preventative Measures

We purposely waited until now to talk about preventative measures, because we felt they would strike home more once our readers had an idea of what to expect if involved in a hostage situation. As we mentioned in Chapter 1, if the hostage takers want you badly enough, they'll find a way to get to you. The key, however, is to make this "way" as expensive as possible in terms of their resources and time. Any measures you and your family take to lessen your "capturability" are going to raise the price of that capture attempt. For example, one of the common security suggestions is to constantly change your routines. [5] "The value of unpredictability can be illustrated by an incident that occurred in pre-revolutionary Iran. Several antigovernment safe houses were discovered by the authorities, who found in one of the houses a list of nearly 200 potential kidnap victims who had been under observation by the terrorists. In every case where the potential victim was unpredictable, the terrorists had crossed his name off the list."

You must develope a security mind-set. Yes, this means YOU as an individual. Between the years of 1970 and 1978, more than half of the 567 Americans kidnapped abroad were businessmen, not military or government personnel. "So what?" you might say. "They had security guards didn't they? Why didn't the guards protect them better?" If the businessmen had been more alert and had practiced the advice their security people had given them, fewer might have been kidnapped. All the King's horses and all the King's men (security specialists) couldn't put Humpty Dumpty (the kidnapped hostage) back together again. If Humpty hadn't sat on the wall in the first place, tempting fate, he wouldn't have fallen off. If a person at risk insists on living a high profile life, he's sitting on the allegorical wall. Don't you sit on it! Follow good security procedures. The following suggestions come from a research and writing project Mike Moak did while attending the Army's Command and General Staff College. They were compiled from several open source military manuals and represent some sound approaches to security. We will discuss measures for the following areas:

- Residential Security
- Family Awareness
- Lowering Your Profile
- Travel Security
- Personal Protection Measures

Then Bob will provide some recommendations against carjacking.

Residential Security

The very first aspect of residential security is the selection of living quarters. Approximately half of your time or more is spent in and around your residence. Almost everything you do from day to day starts or ends in the vicinity of your home. Thus there are a number of aspects to consider when selecting the location of your residence. You should obtain preliminary information from people who are familiar with the area and know which neighborhoods are secure. This information can usually be obtained from Realtors, local police, government authorities, and friends living there. You should begin your consideration of residential security by learning all you can about the neighborhood you have tentatively selected.

Neighborhood Check

The best way to become familiar with a neighborhood is on foot, enabling you to view the entire area. Pay particular attention to the streets (how wide, paved or unpaved, how well maintained), number and kind of vehicles parked along the streets, sidewalks, lighting, pedestrian and vehicular traffic patterns, parks, playgrounds, recreation areas, the existence of public or commercial enterprises intermingled with residential buildings, fire hydrants and police call boxes. The type of residences in the area will give some idea of the income level of the neighborhood. Families with similar income levels frequently share similar life styles, building rapport among neighbors. Note the overall security precautions that people are taking in that neighborhood. Barred windows, security fences, extensive lighting, large dogs, and guards (particularly during the day) may be indicators of a high crime level. As you conduct your neighborhood check, try to keep the mental image of the neighborhood in relation to the rest of the city or town. An area map would be of considerable benefit, for once you have looked at the neighborhood, you should be considering its proximity to police and firefighting facilities, hospitals, shopping facilities, and your place of work. You should familiarize yourself with the routes to all locations you will frequent, ensuring that you would be able to cope with any emergency that may arise.

Crime Level

The level of crime or terrorist activity throughout a community is not uniform. Street crimes can be expected to occur in areas that are used as residences for lower income families where conditions include crowding and congestion. The overall crime rate can be expected to be high in downtown or commercial areas as well as isolated areas. We recommend that these areas be avoided. The local police and residents should be aware of local crime levels in the various areas of your community.

Police Security Capabilities

Your observations of police patrol activity or lack thereof made during your neighborhood check should provide a good indication of the degree of police protection available. Police who take pride in their appearance, the appearance of their vehicle and who make themselves visible to the public in the performance of their duties can usually be relied upon to provide dependable coverage throughout the community. One factor of consideration is the attitude of the government and populace toward other nationals and particularly Americans. A strong anti-American attitude could be a cause to have diminished faith in the local police.

Utilities Services and Protection

The reliability of utility service in any given location should be a primary factor in the selection of a residential site. In many of the lesser developed countries, electricity, running water, indoor plumbing, and telephone service are either not available or are unreliable. Reliability of such services should be determined and in cases where they are not, backup services should be a major consideration. Disruption of services, particularly electricity, would greatly aid an intruder penetrating your residence. Locations of terminal boxes and wiring should be noted. If they are on the outside of the residence and readily available to an intruder, security measures should be developed to protect them.

When terrorists used a lone woman posing as a meter reader to surveil General Dozier's Italian apartment, they violated the Italian utility company's standard operating procedure, which required female meter readers to always travel in pairs. Had Mrs. Dozier known this fact, she might have become suspicious. If you live in a tropical country that practices the custom of Siesta-time, don't expect to see gas or water company workers tearing up the street or erecting barricades during that time. If they are, it may be a setup to entrap you. Get away quickly and report it to the proper authorities.

Access Routes

The greatest danger to your safety exists in the vicinity of your residence. Statistics of kidnappings and assassinations reveal a vast majority occur close to home when the victim is either leaving or returning home. In fact, 80% of all terrorist kidnappings take place while the victim is driving enroute. It is essential that access routes to and from your residence provide sufficient alternatives allowing you to vary your course and avoid attacks. Some considerations should include:

- Clear delineation of street or roadway.
- Sufficient width to allow two cars to pass, even if ve hicles are parked on both sides of the roadway.
- Unobstructed view of the road from your residence.
- Avoiding a residence on a one-way or dead-end street.

Parking

Selection of a residence that provides some means of parking off the street is important. Ideally, a garage that can be locked is the most suitable means of securing your vehicles. Often this luxury will not be available to you. Carports and driveways within a fenced or guarded area will normally suffice. Storage sheds can usually be utilized for storage of bicycles and motorcycles. In the case of a garage, a direct access from the house to the garage is optimum.

Additional Residence Security Measures

Some additional worthwhile security measures are:

- Perimeter Fencing
- Timers for lights

- Smoke alarms and fire extinguishers
- Escape ladders for upper windows
- Secure outside fuse and switch boxes
- Auto-dialers on phones with emergency numbers preprogrammed
- Safe room in house with solid door, lock, emergency supplies, and cell phone / radio communications.
- Weapon available (preferably a shotgun), out of sight and properly stored
- Watchdog (preferably a German Shepherd or a Rotweiler, since they are safest breeds around the fam ily)

Family Awareness

Usually kidnapping attacks occur while the victim is traveling to or from work or at work. This does not mean that people are not targeted in their social, recreational, or residential environments. Although spouses and children have not generally been specific targets of terrorists, they certainly have been targets for criminals. Families should understand they can contribute to the overall level of protection if every member is security conscious. They can help prevent terrorist activities and other criminal acts through their own efforts, and they should be prepared to act in any emergency. Your family's awareness of personal security is the foundation of your protective efforts. Here are three important points:

- Stress the importance of security and the seriousness of the threat to the whole family without causing undue alarm.
- Cultivate mutual concern for security so that all family members are involved with security efforts.
- Establish basic family security procedures.

Each family member should be familiar with the security procedures and techniques. Some common sense precautions, which pertain to all members of the family, are:

- Habitually keep outside doors, windows, and the ga rage closed and locked.
- Keep house keys separate from car keys and maintain accountability.
- Change locks if keys are lost or stolen.
- Never open doors to unscheduled repairmen or strang ers.
- Verify all repair and delivery men. Do not open the door. Have them slide their identification under the door and

then call and verify.

- Do not accept unsolicited packages or other suspicious mail.
- Never consent to requests from telephone repairmen that you not answer your phone.
- Always try to obtain an unpublished and unlisted num ber. Never identify yourself upon answering the phone and never give out any information such as your name and number. Keep a log of all mysterious calls (times, nature of call(s), apparent sex/age of caller, and other distinctions).
- Be alert to all suspicious and unusual activity, and re port everything that happens, regardless of hoe insig nificant it appears to be.
- Develop a family duress code so that family members can warn each other when they are in danger.

Advise children to:

- Avoid isolated streets and play areas.
- Travel and play in groups.
- Never answer a stranger's questions.
- Never go anywhere with a stranger.
- Keep family members informed of their whereabouts.
- Immediately report all attempts to question, annoy, or molest them.
- Note all information possible about unusual incidents.
- Never accept anything from a stranger.
- Ensure that school officials will only release your chil dren to responsible known members of the family or verified designates.
- Do not permit your children to ride public transporta tion unaccompanied.
- Have children escorted to and from school if possible.
- Never leave your children at home unattended.
- Teach your children to scream, "This is not my Daddy (Mommy)!", at the top of their lungs.
- If absent from your residence, have a trusted friend pick up the newspaper and mail, cut the grass, park his car in your driveway, and do other things to give your resi dence the look that someone is at home.

Lowering Your Profile

To lower one's profile, one should consider and practice the following precautions:

- Attempt to blend in with your surroundings.

Americans traveling overseas have a tendency to be loud and obnoxious, drawing much attention to themselves. With the increased terrorist threat, it is important that we learn to blend in with our surroundings like a chameleon. Additionally, as unofficial ambassadors for our country, we do not need to be labeled the "Ugly American". Sometimes it doesn't take much; Bob has a friend who traveled down to Italy for a week's vacation. When US Forces travel in Europe, they must have U.S. Forces license plates and a large U.S.A. decal on their vehicle. That's like waving a big red, white, and blue flag at the Italian Communist element. His car was vandalized and stripped so badly in the week period, it had to be transported back to his home in Heidelberg, Germany via a truck.

- Avoid showing off material wealth. This goes for any one anywhere. If you have a lot of money, don't make an issue of it. People without money resent the rich and may see them as a kidnapping target. Try to live life low key if you don't want unwanted attention.

- Drive an inconspicuous vehicle similar, if not the same, to those common to the area.

- Use unmarked parking spaces and vary where you park.

- Do not place your family name on your car or home.

- Avoid publicity. If you are highlighted in public and you become involved in a hostage situation, media cov erage of the incident may be higher because of your in volvement, affording the hostage taker free and in creased publicity.

- Information about your home, car, family, security ef forts, and activities should only be known by the imme diate family, friends, and security personnel, and only on a need-to-know basis.

- Avoid establishing any daily routines. Being unpredict able is your best defense! Statistics show that by simply avoiding routines and by varying when, where, and how you do daily tasks, you reduce your chances of becom ing the victim of a terrorist attack by 65%.

Recommendations for Survival

The majority of all terrorist attacks, whether assassinations or kidnappings, take place while the victim is in transit. While traveling, there are more precautions you can take to lessen the chance and success for an attack on you or your family.

- Avoid routines while traveling.

- Have a working knowledge of the language of any for eign areas you travel through so that you can call for help.

- Keep a record of your passport number, date and place of issue on a piece of paper in your pocket.

- Never travel with an Israeli entrance or exit stamp in your passport. They will refrain from marking it if you ask.

- Keep any medicines in your hand baggage. Don't put them in your checked baggage where they will be out of reach during a hijacking situation.

- Never carry alcohol or even mild pornography with you on a plane. A fanatic Muslim might take grave of fense. For similar reasons, don't carry political tracts or literature.

- Use curbside luggage check-in whenever possible to stay out of waiting lines in a non-secure area. Spend most of your waiting time within the security area at a res taurant or bar. Don't spend any more time around the loading gate than necessary. Obtain your boarding pass and wait away from the gate until your flight is called. When at the gate, face away from windows and don't sit next to unattended luggage or waste cans.

- Travel in groups when possible.

- Avoid isolated roads, danger areas, civil disturbances, and ugly crowds.

- Be alert and note anyone who appears to be following. If you suspect that you're being followed, walk or drive around the block to see if he's still behind you. Do not antagonize the individual; quickly move to a safe ha ven and report the incident.

- Keep emergency numbers handy and always have the exact change for a phone call.

- Keep your business and family constantly aware of your whereabouts when on a trip.

- Whenever you travel overseas or in a high threat area, ensure all your personal matters are in order. Fill in the contingency plan in the appendix. This won't prevent an attack; however, it will ease your mind that your fam ily will be taken care of in your absence if you are taken hostage.

- On long trips, know the threats in the areas that you visit and travel through.

- Stay at safe, convenient locations on overnight trips. If you want to really be paranoid (and sometimes that may be a necessity in a high risk area), follow these guides as well:

1) Avoid using public transportation when possible; how ever, buses and trains are preferred to taxies.
2) Luggage should be void of markings linking you to your nationality.
3) Patronize reputable hotels only.

- Avoid hotel paging.

- Do not stay in hotel rooms located on the first floor or that are easily accessible from the outside.

- Avoid riding elevators.

- Make reservations in two or more hotels and use an assumed or modified name.

- When in a hotel, note the escape routes.

- Do not discuss travel plans over hotel phones.

Remember, you are only as vulnerable as you allow. While there is no absolute protection against a terrorist or criminal, reasonable safeguards, commensurate with the identified threat to you, can be taken to reduce the likelihood of attack.

Anti-Carjacking Tips

Carjackers prefer to surprise their victims, counting on their victims' sudden fear to incapacitate them. Be careful to anticipate possible situations and to always react with safety and security in mind.

- **KEEP YOUR DOORS LOCKED AND YOUR WIN DOWS SHUT!**
- Always park in well-lit areas.
- Do not park near walls or heavy foliage which can ob scure others' views of you and your vehicle.
- The use of vallet or attended garages is prefered if you are a lone woman.
- Be observant of suspicious people in other cars.
- Ask for a security escort if it's available.
- Listen to your instincts, if they are telling you to run to a busy store.
- When you return to your vehicle, look around, under, and inside it.
- Teach your children these same concepts and to obey you instantly if you say the words, "SECURITY MODE". All instructions after that must be instantly obeyed. Prac tice this!
- When you stop in traffic, always leave enough room to maneuver out of your lane.
- If you are bumped from behind by young males, do not stop and get out. Drive immediately to a police of fire station. Stay in your car and blow your horn for atten tion.
- If you are confronted by an armed carjacker, don't re- sist, unless you fear for your life or your passengers'.
- Call the police immediately. A cell phone is a good thing to have with you in the car.

Be Observant

Learn to be observant and to think on your feet. Try to always be aware of what's going on around you. In urban areas, this is called developing "street-smarts". Experienced Beat-Cops seem to have a sixth-sense for danger and things out of the ordinary. You need to develop this ability for your own needs. Let's say you're walking down the sidewalk and you start to enter a convenience store. As you open the door, you notice that all the customers and clerks are standing quietly, doing nothing. STOP! Are these people involved in a robbery? Don't take a chance. Pivot!

Get out of there fast!

After Bob retired from Army Civil Service in 1993, he went on the road all over the United States presenting workshops to an average of 200 students each weekend for a total of over 10,000 students in two and a half years. He has learned that one of his elderly students in California remembered this advice. She went into a grocery to buy food and cash a check. She came out, stowed her groceries in her car, and walked to the next-door pharmacy to get some prescriptions refilled. She noticed a couple of guys outside watching her as she entered the drug store. When she came out, they were waiting for her outside the door.

"Where ya goin', old lady?"
"To my car."
"We'll just go with ya," and they took her arms, guiding her toward her car. She acted submissive, then she pivoted, jerking away from the thugs, and ran screaming into the drugstore. The police were called, and the guys were caught a couple of blocks away.

The Capture Phase

If you don't immediately determine that a hostage situation is developing, you're far better doing nothing at that time. Don't give the hostage takers reason to single you out as a troublemaker. Don't give them an excuse to make an example out of you. You can best do this by:

- Obey orders!
- Don't speak unless spoken to. Don't whisper to your neighbor.
- Don't look the captors in the eye, they might interpret it as a challenge.
- Don't offer suggestions, they might backfire.
- Don't argue or talk belligerently. Don't try to throw your weight around, you'll lose!
- Don't make any sudden moves, ask to move first.
- Don't try to be humorous, they want to be taken seri

ously.

- Get rid of items that might point you out as one of their enemy. If you are traveling on an official passport or military ID., try to hide them. Most American government travelers travel on their blue tourist passport while enroute and keep official documents well hidden until they reach their destination.
- Keep as calm as possible.

Transport and/or Consolidation Phase

Once the action starts to slow down a little and you sense that the immediate danger is over, consider these aspects:

- Be patient and try to rest.
- Advise on and request special medication or aid that you might need. Point out that you'll be worthless as a hostage if you die or become critically ill.
- If on a plane, follow the flight crew's requests and or ders. Treat the captor well. Be polite without being con descending or subservient.
- Try to develop rapport by reminding them of your hu manity. Show family pictures. Ask them what their cause is, then listen well and don't argue. If they want to take your personal belonging, let them. If the item is really that important, why were you traveling with it in the first place? Your resistance will only single you out.
- Be observant so that you can give as much usable infor mation to the authorities if you are released early or es cape.
- Be prepared to communicate with the outside world if requested. If there is a special code that your family would understand, mentally compose your message ahead of time.
- Start planning your escape. Their guard may lower a little during the transport phase.
- If moved, strain all your senses to try to identify the route and destination. Memorize as much of these sen sations as you can. Make mental notes of all voices, ex ternal sounds, movements, smells, distances, and travel time.

Confinement/Holding

Be prepared for the captor to try to keep you disoriented. Try to keep track of time in any way you can. Make your confinement time count by:

- Keeping physically active,
- Keeping mentally active,

- Visualizing your escape plan in action,
- Setting up communications with other prisoners,
- Asking for reading and writing materials,
- And increasing your spiritual horizons.

Physical Resistance

The following aspects of physical resistance are very important to remember:

- Know your limitations.
- If there is the slightest chance of hesitation or fumbling on your part, you may be better off not trying anything!
- Consider the impact of your actions on your fellow hos tages.
- Don't try to resist at first, wait!

If you must use violence,

- Remember timing is very important.
- Don't give away your true speed, strength, or capabili ties before the time you need them.
- Do not hesitate, go for broke!
- Aim your blows at a point behind the actual target and don't stop till he's down and not moving.
- Strike the most vulnerable points.
- Use weapons whenever possible.
- Be aggressive.
- Take care and think twice if your captor has a weapon.
- Study a street-fighting oriented martial art. Psychologi cal Resistance

The most effective activity you can do to help yourself through a hostage situation is mental. Remember, the most damaging aspect of these incidents is the feeling of overwhelming helplessness. Your mind can be extremely active, doing all kinds of positive things for yourself, and your captors will never know the difference. Expect the following psychological phenomena:

- Initial denial and terror.
- Helplessness, hopelessness, and disorientation.
- The Stockholm syndrome equals positive feelings to ward the hostage taker, negative feelings toward the au thorities and rescuers, positive feeling on the part of the captors toward their victims.
- Hallucinations
- Flow-State experiences during highly charged situations such as the capture or rescue. Once the Stockholm syn

drome has begun to work for you, you might be able to manipulate your captors. Try to set them against one another.

Escape Planning and Execution

There are four types of escapes:

- Individual escape,
- Group escape,
- External force rescue,
- Abductor release.

Before planning an escape, consider:

- Hostage treatment,
- The possibility for eventual release,
- The physical/mental condition of those to participate in the escape attempt,
- The condition of those that may have to stay behind.

A good escape plan should answer these questions:

- How to escape?
- When to escape?
- How to stay free?
- Where to go once initially free?
- How to get there?

To answer these questions, you must gather information and organize it in your mind. Once you have a plan that seems workable, you must:

- Evaluate it and yourself.
- Develop rapport with your captors.
- Assess your captors' routines and look for aspects you can use.
- Perform a gut check as to your willingness to go through with the escape and all that it entails.
- Confront the possibility of confrontation with your cap tors.

Once you gain your initial freedom,

- Blend in with your surroundings.
- Seek help.
- Travel away from the confinement area.
- And consider using a vehicle to make your getaway.

Do whatever you have to do. THE KEY IS TO SURVIVE, AND IT'S OK TO DO THAT!

Incident Termination

There are four types of terminations:

- Abductor release — never turn it down!
- Hostage escape
- Rescue- hit the deck and follow orders!
- Hostage murder/Abductor suicide

Post Incident

Often a few hours of hostage captivity may leave years of emotional scarring. There are many Post-Traumatic Stress Disorder effects. These must be dealt with quickly and professionally. The key is professional counseling with support from family and friends.

In Summary

We have come a long way together. Hostage-Taking is not a pleasant subject; however, the more active a role the public takes in facing its reality, the better chance its victims will have in surviving the experience.

[1] Frank A. Boltz Jr. and Edward Hershey, *Hostage Cop*, McClelland and Stewart, Ltd., 1 979.

[2] Frank A. Boltz Jr., *How to be a Hostage and Live*, Lyle Stuart Inc., 1987.

[3] Neil C. Livingston, *The War Against Terrorism*, D.C. Heath and Company, 1982.

[4] Gayle Rivers, *The War Against the Terrorists: How to Win It*, Stein and Day Publishers, 1986.

[5] Livingston, P. 223.

CHAPTER 12

The Gracia Burnham Interview—5 March, 2003

Martin and Gracia Burnham worked for the New Tribes Mission in the Philippines since 1986. Martin was a missionary bush pilot and Gracia helped in several different aviation support roles. He was the son of missionaries who worked for the same organization in the Philippines and grew up there. Gracia is the daughter of a Pastor in Arkansas. Martin and Gracia's three children, Zach, 11, Mindy, 12, and Jeff, 15, were all born there.

Martin and Gracia were taken hostage by the Abu Sayyef Group, Muslim rebels, on May 27, 2001. On June 7, 2002, Martin was killed and Gracia was wounded in a sudden firefight between government forces and the rebels. The following is a transcript of a telephone interview between the author and Gracia on March 5, 2003. It is interesting to see how much of the advice contained in this book was practiced by the Burnhams. It is also important to note not all stories have a perfect happy ending. There are no guarantees in life, especially when someone hostile to our welfare has control of us, but it is possible to increase one's chances of making it through alive.

Q: Did you or your husband, Martin, ever worry about being targets of terrorists or criminals?

A: There was one time when the embassy sent a couple of Marines to Mindanao to talk with us. There'd been some talk somewhere along the lines of a pilot in Mindanao who was targeted. They told Martin to take precautions. He was supposed to vary his way to the airport every day; try not to keep a schedule that anyone could by watching our house know what time he left for work or anything like that. We were supposed to keep an eye out in the neighborhood for anything strange. We heeded all those warnings; we really did. Every time the State Department would issue some kind of travel advisory for anything in the Philippines, we really did pay close and careful attention to those. We stayed away from hot spots. We stayed aware of what was going on around us, but no, we never were fearful along the way that something was going to happen. We were living on Luzon, and we always thought if we had any trouble, it would be the communist guerrillas, rather than the Muslims. We just happened to be at the wrong place at the wrong time.

Q: How were you taken hostage?

A: We had gone to the island of Palawan. Martin had some flying to do there, because the normal pilot there had had to leave suddenly. His father died, and to get to the funeral, he and his family had left suddenly. We work with people who live out in the bush where there are no roads. They were dependent on the planes. Martin had just gotten home from meetings in the US regarding his duties, and I knew he needed a little time to rest up before he started in on his heavy flying. I called Palawan and asked some co-workers where a good place would be for Martin to rest up for a day. They told us about this little island off the coast of Palawan where the whole island was a resort—a really nice place. When they told me the price, I almost backed out because it was too much. But, they booked us in, and it was a beautiful resort.

Just before dawn the next morning after we arrived on the island, there was a hammering on the door. By the time Martin had pulled some clothes on, three guys had burst in with M-16s. They took us and eighteen other people off on a speed boat into the ocean.

Q: How did they get you away from the resort?

A: By the time they were done, they had cleared out the cottages. The cottages were out over the water, built on stilts, and they cleared those out. There were twenty of us—we two and one other American. The rest were middle-class to wealthy Filipinos and Chinese businessmen. They loaded us onto a speed boat, and we headed out into the ocean.

Q: And so they just knew they had a target population. They weren't aware of any individuals?

A: They were not targeting certain people. They knew the more wealthy went to Dos Palmas. You know, I almost picked up the phone and called my friends when I found out how much it was. It was like $100 a day per person, which was a lot more than I had ever spent before or would spend. I was just going to ask if there was a cheaper place in town for us to stay. So the quality of people who stay at that resort are people with money.

Q: How were you treated initially?

A: Fairly well. They burst into the room, and I didn't have clothes on. They were yelling, "Go, go, go!" They took Martin out right away. To get control of Martin, just as he was stepping out through the door, they used a gun to butt him at the nape of the neck, in the back, just so they were sure he would obey. We heard that each of the men and some of the women they did that to. When one of the guys saw I wasn't dressed yet, that I was still pulling clothes on, he just told me, "Hurry, hurry, hurry!" He let me get clothes on. So, initially, we were treated well.

Q: Did you ever know why some hostages were killed and some were set free?

A: To my knowledge there was only one killed . . . that's not really true. There were twenty who were taken from Dos Palmas, the name of the resort, and later there were some boys from a coconut plantation taken, and some of those boys tried to escape and were shot. There were also some employees from the Dos Palmas resort who were beheaded late one night. No, I never really understood why they chose them. Aside from the fact that two of them were security guards. I did hear one of the Abu Sayyaf say that often someone who was ex-military would take a security job. But, these were kids. They weren't former soldiers or anything. There was really no need for the rebels to kill them.

The American who was killed—they viewed him as a bad guy from the very beginning. They found drugs in his room, although they were prescription drugs. He was in his room with a person who wasn't his wife at the resort. They immediately explained their code of modesty, not only for women, but for men also. We tried as much as we could to comply with that. This other guy from California just didn't clue into that. The Muslims have this code—they have rules of what a good person is and what a bad person is, and it's just a big bunch of rules which they eventually broke themselves. There is a deep seated code of right and wrong.

Even though we were Christian missionaries, we fit into that code. Martin was a family man and he was nice. He didn't drink; and he didn't do drugs. Another thing, they hated rock music, but of course they listened to it every time they could tune it in on their radios. Morally we fit their code better than that businessman from California, and that's why I really think he lost his life.

Q: How were you kept captive and where? In the jungle? In buildings? Were they moving you around all the time? Was it in caves?

A: It was in the jungle. They would send scouts out for an hour or so, and come back and other guys would go out. If they thought we were in a safe area and there was no military around, we would set up camp and stay there. I recall being in one place almost six weeks I think. Sometimes we would remain in a place for two or three weeks and sometimes just a few days. If they knew the military was near, we kept movin'. We just tramped through the jungle.

Q: How did they feed you?

A: Well, there were enough sympathizers on the island of Basilan. Now, I can't tell you if most of the people on Basilan . . . I can't tell you the ratio between Muslims and Christians. I know there are a lot of Christians, which is what they called anyone who was not a Muslim. There were enough Muslims in the area, that the guys would go out and order rice by the 50-pound sack. They would go out the next night and pick it up, along with coffee and sugar and anything else they needed . . . and sardines was a big thing.

As long as the money lasted, there was always people willing to sell to these guys. When there wasn't money, there were lots of farms on Basilan, and when I say farms, it's not like what we would think of. A family has gone into the forest and cleared a place and planted fruit trees. There would be green bananas and coconuts and maybe some root crops just growing haphazardly. They would call that a farm. We would help ourselves to whatever happened to be growing there.

Q: Now I know that Martin had a significant amount of weight loss. Was this because of the diet?

A: Oh, for sure, or from the lack of. The lack of food—yeah.

Q: I presume you lost a good amount of weight too.

A: Well, I wish I could say I had. By the time I got home and could stand on the leg that was wounded, I weighed the same as when I went in, so my fat must have turned to muscle, I guess, with all that hiking in the jungle.

Q: Did you ever plan what you might do if given an opportunity to escape?

A: Ah yes, we decided that we wouldn't try unless we were pretty sure we could do it. That opportunity never presented itself clearly to us. Thinking back, there were two different times we could have been able to sneak away during the night. On the other hand, we didn't know if they had people stationed down the hill or not. Our whole thinking was, if we stay here, something might happen and we might get to go home to our kids. If we try to bolt and fail, our kids aren't going to have parents. This was pretty much what we thought.

If we ever had gotten away, we would have followed a river all the way down to the coast. That's all we knew to do. Lots of times there was so much vegetation and trees in the jungle, you couldn't tell where the sun was rising or setting. The other thing was, the Abu Sayyaf are very successful against the military because they know the terrain. They grew up there. They knew the woods and they knew the trails. We would have been at a great disadvantage had we ever tried to get away.

Q: Did you ever think about what might happen if a rescue attempt took place? Did you ever plan for what you might do if you were ever rescued?

A: We had decided . . . we had talked about every time the guns would start up . . . there were seventeen gun battles. Martin died in our seventeenth fight. We were just going to drop to the ground. We knew that we probably wouldn't get the chance to crawl toward the military. We certainly didn't trust the Philippine military. There's no such thing with them as selective gun fire. We knew that from experience after the first few encounters we had with them. They just raked the area with M-16 fire, so we knew we weren't going to have a chance. We knew there wouldn't be snipers who knew what they were doing should we crawl toward them. Our only chance was that they would just leave us lying on the ground. So we didn't spend a whole lot of time planning anything, because we knew sooner or later we weren't going to get missed by those bullets that the military were spraying our way. We knew our luck was going to run out. I don't really believe in luck.

Q: Was Martin killed by a military bullet, or did your captors purposely kill him?

A: No, he was killed when the military came over the hill. I think we surprised them. We had stopped for the day, because it was going to start raining. One of the unwritten rules of the military was that you don't fight in the rain. We had just set up our hammocks and put up little shelters . . . we called them *poldas*. They were made out of plastic that you put over your hammock. We had just gotten ready for an afternoon rest, and the military came over the hill and there we were. They just opened fire. They shot all three hostages.

Q: They . . . the military?

A: The military . . . It doesn't really matter, 'cause the bad guys were the Abu Sayyaf. That was the other thing Martin and I would talk about every few days. We would remind ourselves who the good guys were and who the bad guys were, because it was really hard for us to think of the Filipino military as the good guys. If they knew where we were, they would lob artillery at us from ten miles away. We thought, how can they plan on rescuing hostages if they're shooting artillery at us. So, we knew our situation, but we wanted to remind ourselves who the good guys were and who the bad guys were.

Q: Were you kept together as a couple or were you kept separate from one another?

A: We were always together.

Q: How did you deal with the tedium of captivity?

A: We did a lot of talking. We talked about things that happened to us in our childhood—stories of growin' up. Martin told me about living in Kansas with his cousins, and the stupid things they did on their grandpa's farm. The tree houses they built. If we finished telling all the stories we could think of and our brains were just fried and we didn't want to think up any more, we would just tell the same stories to each other over and over.

We sang a lot too. I couldn't believe all the songs Martin remembered. He'd start in on some James Taylor song that I didn't even know he knew, but the amazing thing was he knew all the words to the whole songs. I'm a pastor's daughter; I knew all the words in the hymn books, so we spent a lot of time singin'. Now they didn't appreciate a women being heard, so my singing was in this tiny, whispery voice. They didn't mind Martin singing loud enough for some of them to hear, if we were in a safe place. If we weren't sure that we were in a safe place, we just kinda sang in our heads and everybody kept the noise down of course.

Q: When you were together as a family before the hostage taking, did you ever discuss with your children what to do if the family was split apart by any disaster or a hostage situation?

A: No, but we knew what our mission would do. We had had some training. It was called a contingency seminar. A guy had come who used to be in the Special Forces in the military, I believe. He had come and told us about hostage situations and our mission organization had said, if anyone was taken hostage, that the nearest kin would be evacuated immediately from the country. So we knew what would happen to our children.

Q: What advice would you give to other missionaries or others in harm's way in the world?

A: For what it's worth . . . I guess my only credibility is that I lived in the jungle for a year, but I don't claim to be an expert on this at all. Here's what I would say: right away when you're taken, they say, those first few moments are the critical ones . . . you comply totally with what they say during the first few moments. Right after that, you need to catch the eye of someone and let them know you're human. I remembered that, and I think that really may have helped. They'd taken us from our beds and everybody needed to go to the bathroom, but nobody wanted to say anything. Finally I just stood up on the speed boat and said, "We have a need here, and we're going to have to do something." I think letting them know we were humans and needed something helped.

Martin was very kind. If there was anyway he could help anyone, he did it. He fixed short-wave radios. He showed the guys how to set the watches they'd stolen. He showed them how to make a battery pack and they finally got a solar panel in and he showed them how to charge a battery pack, so we could keep communications going with the satellite phones. If somebody had a headache and we had medicine, he would share it with them. He was just very kind and not confrontational. He did most anything he could to not confront. I think that really helped our situation.

Yeah, talk to your family before hand, but on the other hand, what you think is a really great plan before you become a hostage, is probably going to change within about ten minutes after you actually become one. Your opinion is probably going to change really fast. We knew that New Tribes Mission wouldn't pay a ransom, and we agreed with that. As soon as we were taken hostage though, we wanted someone to pay a ransom for us. We really thought through all this ransom stuff and decided the person who pays the ransom isn't the bad guy, it's the person doing the extorting that is the bad guy.

My advice is: you can plan; you can read all the books; and you can go to all the seminars and be ready; but nothing's going to prepare you for a hostage situation except a really close walk with God. What you believe deep down in your heart is what's going to get you through. If you see yourself as a part of the plan of God Almighty and throw yourself on him, you're going to have a whole different world view as to whether you can get through this situation or not.

APPENDIX

A FILL-IN-THE-BLANKS FAMILY CONTINGENCY PLAN FOR HOSTAGE SITUATIONS

The authors grant the reader permission to photocopy any and all pages of this book's appendix, or you can download a copy for free at www.-----.

Fill in those blanks and areas applicable to your family's needs and keep it on hand. We recommend that the family discuss this plan amongst themselves until everyone knows how they will carry-on if one or more are ever taken hostage. Keep your completed plan in a safe but convenient place, such as a fire-resistant file box in the house. It may also be useful for a trustee, a designated family guardian, or the family lawyer to keep a copy on file as well. This plan may prove useful in any number of emergency situations.

I. PERSONAL DATA AS OF (date)

1. Current photos of each family member are located in the envelope at TAB A. The name and age of each family member are written upon the backs of their respective photos.

2. FAMILY MEMBERS PHONE NUMBERS

NAME	RELATIONSHIP	HOME/WORK	BIRTH DATE	ADDRESS
a.				
b.				
c.				
d.				
e.				
f.				
g				
h.				
i.				

3. EMERGENCY POINTS OF CONTACTS

RELATIONSHIP	NAME	PHONE NO.	ADDRESS
a. Family Lawyer			
b. Family Doctor			
c. Insurance Agent			
d. Financial Trustee			
e. Guardian(s)			
f.			
g.			
h.			
i.			
j.			
k.			

A-2

4. COMMUNICATIONS: If one of the family is taken hostage, the following key words or signs will be used to communicate true conditions in any statements made on audio, video, or written media:

MEANING	**WORD**	**SIGN**
I'M OK!		
I'M SAYING THIS UNDER DURESS!		
I'M LOCATED IN:		
A CITY		
THE COUNTRY		
AN APARTMENT		
A HOUSE		
A SCHOOL		
A CHURCH/MOSQUE		
A HOSPITAL		
I'M LOCATED IN THE:		
NORTH		
SOUTH		
EAST		
WEST		
CENTER		
I'M IN IMMINENT DANGER!		
I LOVE YOU!		

5. CHAIN OF COMMAND:

If Mom and Dad are both taken hostage, injured, or killed, ______________________ is in charge, then __________________, then ________________________.

6. PLAN OF ACTION:

Those of the family not captured or disabled will meet at. They will travel by means of to __________ where they will set up house. If both parents are taken,____________will insure that the rest of the family stays together and helps each other as much as possible. The family's finances are covered in paragraphs _____ and TABs _________ of this plan

Copies of important legal documents may be found at TABs . More details of travel procedures may be found at TAB E. Information to help the Family Guardian may be found at TAB F.

7. RANSOM DIRECTIONS: (Mention any funds, insurance, and procedures you want used in case someone is kidnapped.)

8. GENERAL: Information required for the family to maintain its existence can be found at TABs G-K and N. Information on Dwelling and Vehicle shut-downs can be found at TAB L and, for maintenance of the same, TAB M.

9. DISPOSITION OF THIS PLAN:

A copy of this plan will be left with:

NAME PHONE# ADDRESS

1 0. LEGACY:

In case the worst happens, the best piece of advice I can leave with those who continue on is:

DATE: NAME:

SIGNATURE:

A-4

TAB A: FAMILY PHOTOS

STAPLE ENVELOPE OF PHOTOS HERE

TAB B: MEDICAL HISTORIES 1 FAMILY MEMBERS

NAME	SEX	BIRTHDATE	BLOOD TYPE	ALLERGIES	PHYSICIAN
a.					
b.					
c.					
d.					
e.					
f.					
g.					
h.					

PHYSICIANS

	NAME	SPECIALTY	PHONE	ADDRESS
a.				
b.				
c.				
d.				

A-6

TAB C: WILL

STAPLE COPY OF CURRENT WILLS BEHIND THIS PAGE

TAB D: POWERS OF ATTORNEY

(You should include such powers that a spouse or guardian would require to assume legal leadership of the family. Powers for the financial trustee and the family lawyer should be included. Make a list of these documents on this page and staple them behind it.)

TAB E: TRAVEL PROCEDURES

(Include any instructions necessary to get the family from where they are to where they may have to live until the family is reunited. You could include approximate fares, mileages, transportation means, routes, maps, time tables, a travel budget, location of passports, and shot records. If you are overseas, a loading plan as to what to take and what to pack it in should be written.)

TAB F: INFORMATION FOR THE FAMILY GUARDIAN

(If you have appointed a relative or close friend as the legal guardian of your children in case both parents are taken or indisposed, include all the pertinent instructions and specific information about each family member. Include discipline problems to watch for, talents that need to be encouraged, personal likes and dislikes, and anything else you feel important to pass on.)

TAB G: DISPOSITION OF FAMILY PETS

(If you would have to get rid of any pets because they are too much to travel with, too hard to maintain, or too expensive to feed, you should provide instructions as to whom they should be given or how they should be sold. If they are to be kept, provide care and feeding instructions.)

TAB H: DISPOSITION OF BUSINESS INTERESTS

(Provide instructions on how your interests in sole proprietorships, partnerships, and corporations should be protected, handled, and/or liquidated.)

TAB I: DISPOSITION OF ASSETS

If you would have to liquidate assets such as bonds, stock, savings, loans, etc. to provide immediate cash for the family's survival or for a ransom demand, provide those instructions here. If you have a financial trustee, provide him this guidance and sign and date it.

Asset	Interest Rate	Location	Acquired. Date	Acquired Price
a.				
b.				
c.				
d.				
e.				
f.				
g.				
h.				

TAB J: DISPOSITION OF LIABILITIES

List liabilities in the order of priority you wish them paid.

Liability	Account #	Payment	To Whom	Payment Date	Payoff Date
a.					
b.					
c.					
d.					
e.					
f.					
g.					
h.					

TAB K: INSURANCE

Policy Type	Policy#	Coverage	Insurance Co.	Agent/Phone

TAB L: SHUTTING DOWN THE HOUSE/ APARTMENT/ VEHICLES

(List instructions for closing up the house or apartment if you have to move away. These should include how to turn off the water, gas, and electricity, how to winterize it, and how to secure it. Explain how to clean out refrigerators and any other important cleaning instructions.

List the disposition of any extra vehicles not needed in the family. If vehicles are to be stored, explain how you want the oil and other fluids drained, putting them up on blocks, etc.)

TAB M: MAINTAINING THE HOME / VEHICLES

(Provide detailed lists of those daily, weekly, monthly and yearly chores that are required to maintain your home and vehicles. Include directions on things such as turning on or off the furnace, when to change its fflters, how often to put salt in the water softener, who to call for different things breaking down, how often to check the oil, water, and battery acid in the car, and all the other details you would normally handle if you were there.)

TAB N: SHOPPING INSTRUCTIONS

(If you want your family to purchase food, clothes, etc., suggest where to shop for each type of item, how to do it, and how much to spend on what.)

TAB O and onward:

Anything else you want to use to provide information and guidance

BIBLIOGRAPHY

ARTICLES

Dane, Leila Finlay, PhD., "The Iran Hostage Wives: Long Term Crisis Coping", *Dissertation Abstracts Internationat Vol.* 45(11-B), P. 3614-3615,May1985.

Glass, Charles, "Kidnapped In Beruit", *The Readers' Digest*, April 1988, (Condensed from *Rolling Stone Magazine*)

Hillman, Robert G. M.D., "The Psychopathology of Being Held Hostage", *American Journal of Psychiatry*, Vol 138 No.9, September 1981.

Kentsmith, David K. M.D., "Hostages and Other Prisoners of War", *Military Medicine*, Vol.147, November 1982.

Siegal, Ronald K., PhD, "Hostage Hallucinations: Visual Imagery Induced by Isolation and Life-Threatening Stress", *The Journal of Nervous and Mental Disease*, Vol 172, No.5, 1984.

Simon, Robert I., M.D. and Blum, Robert A, M.D., "After the Terrorist Incident: Psychotherapeutic Treatment of Former Hostages", *American Journal of Psychotherapy*, Vol. XLI, No.2, April 1987.

Solomon, Victor Martin, PhD., "Hostage Psychology and the Stockholm syndrome: Captive, Captor, and Captivity", *Dissertation Abstracts International*, Vol. 43(4-B), October 1982.

"Special Forces Prisoner of War", *Combat Mission Magazine*, Vol.1, Issue 4, Nov 88.

Strentz, Thomas, "Negotiating with the Hostage-Taker Exhibiting Paranoid Schizophrenic Symtoms", *Journal of Police Science and Administration*, Vol 14, No.1,1986.

"Terrorism Counteraction A823", *Atlanta Georgia FBI File Case*,1985/86.

Tobias, Manuel David, PhD., "An Experimental Study of Self-Esteem and Cognitive Dissonance Reduction in Minority Males Who Are Released Early From A Hostage Situation", *Dissertation Abstracts International*, Vol. 41(9-B), March 1981.

Turner, James T., "Factors Influencing the Development of the Hostage Identification Syndrome", *Political Psychology*, Vol. 6, No. 4,1985.

Wesselius, Cassie L., M.D., LCDR MC USNR, and Sarno, James V., FBI Special Agent, "The Anatomy of a Hostage Situation", *Behavioral Sciences and the Law*, Vol 1, No.2, 1983.

McGoey, Chris E., "Carjacking", http://www.crimedoctor.com/carjacking.htm, 2002.

BOOKS

Boltz, Frank A.Jr. and Hershey, Edward, *Hostage Cop*, McClelland and Stewart Ltd.,1979.

Boltz, Frank A. Jr., *How To Be A Hostage and Live*, Lyle Stuart Inc.,1987.

Livingston, Neal C., *The War Against Terrorism*, D.C. Heath and Co.,1982

Matsakis, Aphrodite PhD, *Vietnam Wives*, Woodbine House, 1988.

McFadden, Treaster, & Carroll, *No Hiding Place*, The New York Times Company,1981.

Netanyabu, Benjamine, *Terrorism: How the West Can Win the Global Battle*, The Jonathan Institute,1986..

Random House College Dictionary, Random House, Revised Edition,1982.

Rivers, Gayle, *The War Against Terrorists: How To Win It*, Stein and Doubleday Publishers,1986.

Schreiber, Jan, *The Ultimate Weapon*, William Morrow and Company,1978.

Spear, Robert K., *Hapkido: The Integrated Fighting Art*, Unique Publications,1988.

Kramen, Alissa J.; Massey, Kelly R.; Timm, Howard W., *Guide for Preventing and Responding to School Violence*, Int. Assoc. of Chiefs of Police, 2001.

Resources

Books by Bob Spear:

STAY ALIVE! Survival Tactics for Hostages
Updated from his 1989 version, *Surviving Hostage Situations,* this book explains in detail how to live through one of the most terrifying experiences anyone can have. **$16.50 at www.sharpspear.com or use the form on page 208.**

Hapkido: The Integrated Fighting Art
Learn the specifics of one of the world's most deadly fighting arts by its American pioneer. Bob's abilities as a teacher of this art since the early 1970s make this complex subject easy to understand. This broad-brush overview will acquaint you with the essential knowledge of one of the world's deadliest fighting arts. Hapkido was designed for the street and battlefield. You too can know what some of the world's deadliest fighters know—the many ways of bending, folding, and mutilating the human body. This is why many of America's special operations warriors have studied Hapkido—it really works! **$14.95 at www.sharpspear.com or use the form on page 208.**

Military Knife Fighting
You may never need to fight for your life with a knife, but . . . wouldn't be nice to know how if you do?Learn how to use what resides in every kitchen to protect yourself or a loved one. **$16.95 at www.sharpspear.com or use the form on page 208.**

Video Training Tapes by Bob Spear

Deadly Three-Way Combo — Robert K. Spear Teaches:
Three one-hour-long videos featuring Bob and his son, Patrick, demonstrating easy-to-do and oh-so-effective techniques for your safety and security. What if someone pulled a knife on you, or a gun, or tried to hit you with a club? Would you know what to do? Could you survive the attack?

Defenses Against Weapons Attacks--Featuring knife, pistol, and stick defenses. As always, these are combat-proven, easy, and sensible to effectively use. They have saved numerous lives and are easy to learn, nor are they strength-dependent--meaning an 83-year-old grandmother can do them (and some have).

Offensive Use of Weapons--How to effectively use knives, flashlights, nightsticks, and walking canes. Ladies, wouldn't it be nice to know how to effectively use the weapons at hand in the kitchen? Wouldn't you like to be able to use them while not being afraid your assailant might take them away to use against you?

Metal flashlights and short clubs are handy to carry in the car. You never know when you might need to defend yourself from a roadraging maniac.

Walking canes are a weapons system in the Korean art of Hapkido that dates back to 1,200 AD. Learn how they can be used to strike, poke, lever, and trap an opponent's attack. These techniques are awesome and yet are so easy to do; you'll be amazed!

Fighting in Close and Confined Spaces--Releases from chokes, hugs, locks, fighting on the floor, in cars, in bars, and up against walls. It's a little-known fact that 85% of fights end up with the combatants rolling around on the ground. Could you effectively fight from there? These are techniques not found in traditional karate classes, and yet they address some of the most common threats.

We strongly believe everyone should study all three tapes in order to have a well-rounded knowledge of self defense. This is why we have packaged them together as a set. Normally they would sell for $50 each; however, we have lowered the price for the set of all three to only $97.50, so more people can afford them.**Get all three for $97.50 (a $150 value) at www.sharpspear.com or use the form on page 208.**

Senior Citizen Self-Defense Video and Training Manual
The easiest, yet most devastating techniques ANYONE CAN DO to keep themselves and their families safe from attackers. Bob's recommendations on how to turn many household items into deadly weapons have got to be seen to be believed. Seventh Degree Black Belt Bob is known internationally as a martial arts theorist. His manual explains the reasons techniques work with words and pictures so you'll be able to use them with confidence. His one-hour video takes you through a step-by-step process which will teach ANYONE to defend herself with humor and interesting details and stories. Over 11,000 students throughout the world love his teaching style. The lives of a number of people have been saved because of his training. **$29.95 at www.sharpspear.com or use the form on page 208.**

Bob is available for lectures, workshops, and speeches to your companies and organizations. Contact him at sharpspear@lvnworth.com or call 913-772-8253.

Photocopy this page and fill out the copy to order by mail.

Send To: Sharp Spear Enterprises
410 Delaware
Leavenworth, KS 66048

Qty	Item	Price	SubTotal
	STAY ALIVE Book	$16.50	
	Hapkido Book	$14.95	
	Military Knife Fighting Book	$16.95	
	Three-Way Video Combo	$97.50	
	Senior Citizen Book & Video	$29.95	
		SubTotal	
		Kansas Residents Only Sales Tax 7.3%	
		S&H	$6
		Total	

Name on Credit Card ____________________

Address ____________________

City ____________________

State ________ ZIP ____________________

Visa ________ Master Card ________ Discover ________

Card # ____________________ Expiration Date ________

Email (if we need to contact) ____________________